EYES
OF TEXAS
TRAVEL
GUIDE

Hill Country/Permian Basin Edition

EYES OF TEXAS TRAVEL GUIDE

Hill Country/Permian Basin Edition

By Ray Miller

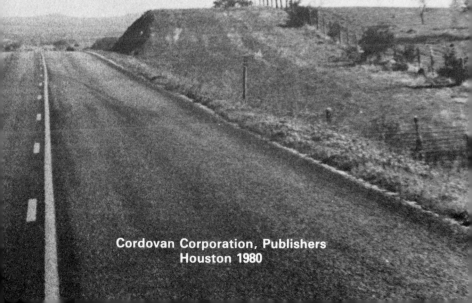

Cordovan Corporation, Publishers
Houston 1980

EYES OF TEXAS TRAVEL GUIDE
Hill Country/Permian Basin Edition
First Printing September 1980

Library of Congress Catalog Number: 80-68868
ISBN: 0-89123-070-X
0-89123-071-8 pbk

Cover design: Russell Jumonville
Maps: Anita Schmoekel
Production art: Ginny Bliss

We dedicate this book to the owners and managers of KSAT TV, San Antonio, KTVV, Austin, KMID TV, Midland, KTAB TV, Abilene, KIII TV, Corpus Christi, KBMT TV, Beaumont, and especially, KPRC TV, Houston. The television program that inspired the "EYES OF TEXAS TRAVEL GUIDES" never would have happened without the interest and support of these out-standing broadcasters.

We are also indebted to the Texas State Historical Commission; the Texas State Library; the Texas Department of Parks and Wildlife; the Texas Department of Highways and Public Transportation; the Institute of Texan Cultures; the Houston Public Library; and the historical organizations in these 38 counties; to Bob Gray and Michelle Browne of the Cordovan Corporation for their assistance; and to Valda Follis for bringing order to the manuscript.

Ray Miller and the staff of "THE EYES OF TEXAS"
Houston
March 1980

Contents

Foreword

Texas is a land of wondrous sights and countless historic landmarks. This is the only state that was a nation. The story of Texas' evolution from a minor Spanish colonial possession to the proud present is a story full of colorful and dramatic events and fascinating personalities.

It is doubtful whether any one Texan has seen or ever will see all the sights worth seeing in Texas. It is not likely that any one Texan knows or ever will know all the details of our rich history. But many of us have learned more than we might otherwise have known by watching the "Eyes of Texas" television programs.

Ray Miller and his colleagues have brought to our attention many historic places, famous personalities, unsung heroes and unusual events over the past dozen years. The "Eyes of Texas" has made old Texans even more proud of their heritage and it has given many new Texans an understanding of the sources of this pride all Texans share.

The "Eyes of Texas" is a service to Texas and Texans and these travel guides are an extension of this service, combining some history with information about what there is to be seen in various parts of the state. The author says he hopes this edition will make Texans want to see more of the Texas Hill Country and Permian Basin. I hope so, too.

Allan Shivers,
Governor of Texas,
1949-1957.

The Texas State Capitol is the most imposing landmark in Austin and the biggest state capitol building in the country. The legislature traded 3 million acres of public land for it.

Introduction

This book is the fourth in the series of travel guides the viewers of "THE EYES OF TEXAS" television program urged us to produce. This volume covers the Hill Country and the southern end of the High Plains. It covers the cities of Austin, San Angelo, Big Spring, Midland and Odessa. It is the area drained by the Colorado River and its tributaries, the Pedernales, Llano, San Saba and Concho.

People have been living in this area for thousands of years. But the early people apparently all were nomads. They left little evidence of their culture beyond a few rock paintings and thousands of arrow and spear points. The Comanche Indians moved down into this area from the northern plains in the 1700s and displaced the earlier Indian inhabitants.

The Comanches were related to the Shoshoni tribe. They learned to catch and ride the wild horses descended from the animals the early Spanish explorers brought to this part of the world. The Comanches were fierce and fearless and superb horsemen. They contested with the Spanish and the Mexicans and the Texans for control of this territory. The contest finally ended only about a hundred years ago. Part of this part of Texas was part of the last frontier.

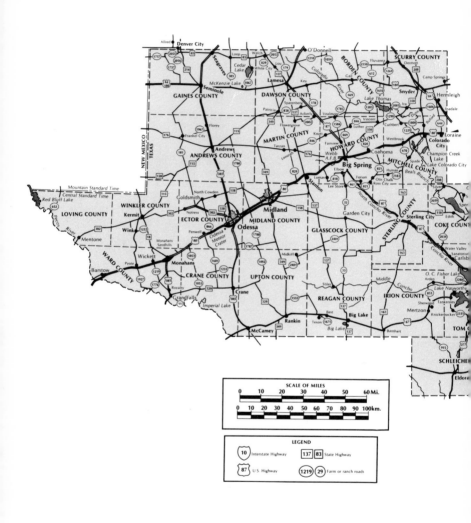

SCALE OF MILES

0   10   20   30   40   50   60 Mi.

0 10 20 30 40 50 60 70 80 90 100km.

LEGEND

(10) Interstate Highway   137 83 State Highway

(87) U.S. Highway   (1219) (29) Farm or ranch roads

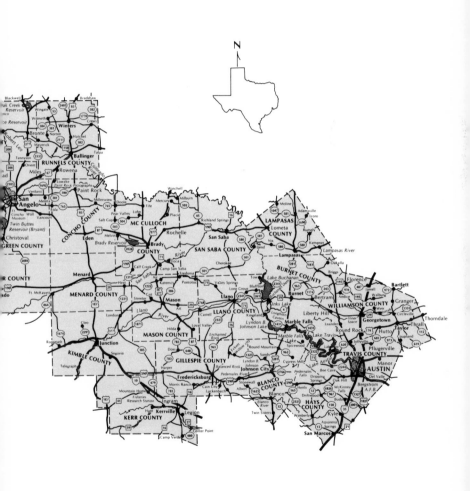

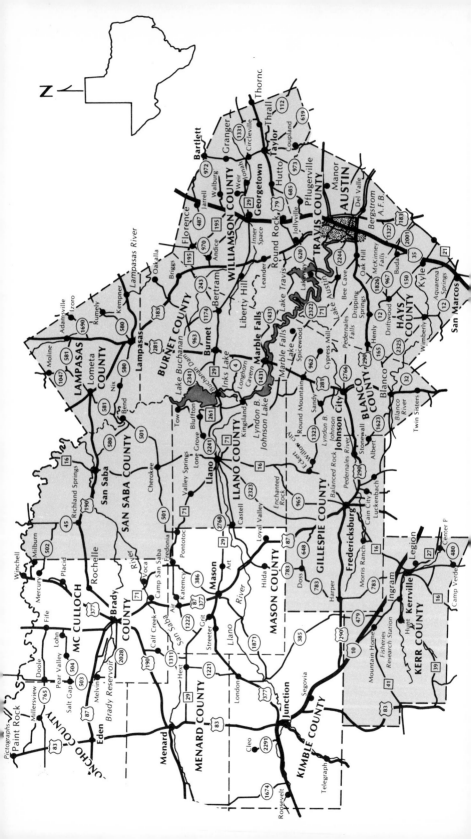

Austin and the hills

Travis, Williamson, Burnet, Lampasas,
San Saba, Llano, Gillespie, Kerr, Blanco
and Hays counties.

Austin was created to be the capital of the Republic of Texas. It has become one of the most gracious and congenial cities in North America.

Austin is the gateway to the Hill Country resort area. The dams the Lower Colorado River Authority has built to control flooding and generate electricity have created some of the most popular lakes in the state. Thousands of Texans and people from faraway places have built summer homes and retirement homes in the hills around these lakes.

Lyndon Baines Johnson was born here, and he died here. The LBJ Ranch and the late president's library and boyhood home are here.

Some of the early German settlements are here.

Willie Nelson is here sometimes, and Luckenbach is nowhere but here.

Heroic representations like this mural in the lobby of the Texas State Library Building on the Capitol grounds may convey the impression that the principal figures in the Texas struggle for independence were friends with common goals. They actually had major differences and the city of Austin is the result of one of the differences. Sam Houston was happy to have the capital of the Republic in Houston while he was president. Mirabeau B. Lamar wanted to move the capital when he succeeded Houston as president. The village that became Austin was built during Lamar's administration, in 1839, and designated the capital in January, 1840.

TRAVIS COUNTY

The city of Austin ranks high on nearly every list of agreeable American cities. The city is named for the colonist Stephen F. Austin. It is the capital of Texas, the county seat of Travis County, and the home of the main unit of the University of Texas. The location on the Colorado River, near the center of the state, where the level plains of southeast Texas blend into the Edwards Plateau, is both pleasant and appropriate. It has always been pleasant, but it has not always been considered appropriate by everybody.

The government of the Republic of Texas decided in 1839 to establish a city to be the capital of the new nation. Mirabeau B. Lamar was president at the time. He was familiar with this area because he had hunted buffalo here, and he steered the capital site selection committee here. The area was on the ragged edge of civilization then. The earliest settlers came from the Stephen F. Austin colony at Bastrop.

The original plan of Austin set aside the ground where the Capitol now stands to be the site of the capitol building. But the first temporary capitol was built at what is now the intersection of Colorado and Eighth. The Senate and the House of Representatives of the Republic met in this log building from 1840 until Houston moved the government out of Austin in 1842. Sessions of the Texas legislature were held here between 1845 and 1853.

The first settler was Reuben Hornsby. He came in 1832 and settled about eight miles east of the present city of Austin. The late baseball star, Rogers Hornsby, was one of the first settler's descendants. The ball player is buried in the Hornsby family cemetery off Farm Road 969. William Barton came in 1837 and settled on Barton Creek at the place that has been known as Barton Springs ever since.

Four families were living around a log stockade on the north bank of the Colorado when the capital site selection committee came here. The stockade had been built by Joseph Harrell. He apparently was the host for the buffalo hunt that gave Mirabeau Lamar his favorable impression of the area. The Harrell stockade was approximately where the Congress Avenue Bridge is today. The settlement was called Waterloo. It was hardly a name to appeal to a president whose middle name was Buonaparte. The Congress already had decided, anyway, that the name of the capital city would be Austin. So the name was changed, and Edwin Waller was appointed to lay out a town and build some public buildings. Waller was

1

2

3

1) Mirabeau Lamar was one of the heroes of the Battle of San Jacinto. Sam Houston promoted him from private to colonel on the eve of the battle and gave him command of the Texas cavalry. Lamar was vice president during Sam Houston's first term as president of the Republic, but they had many differences and Lamar reversed some of Houston's major policies when he succeeded Houston as president.

2) Sam Houston complained that Austin was too far out on the frontier to be a capital city. But some Texans thought Houston opposed the move mostly because of a vain attachment to the city that was named for him. Houston was elected president again at the end of Lamar's term in 1841. He moved the government back to Houston and then to Washington-on-the-Brazos. The government did not return to Austin until Texas became a state in 1845.

3) The President's House was a two-story frame building, painted white. Mirabeau Lamar lived here, but the place was abandoned when Sam Houston moved the government away from Austin in 1842. The house burned in 1847. The St. Mary's Academy occupied the site for many years after that.

You can park your car all day for $1.75 on the site where President Mirabeau B. Lamar lived. This block has been a parking lot since the old St. Mary's Academy was torn down. Austin has more historical markers than any other city in Texas. But there is no marker on the site of the original Executive Mansion.

one of the signers of the Declaration of Independence. He became the first mayor of Austin.

Waller arrived in Austin in May of 1839 with 200 workmen. They set up a construction camp on the creek they named for Waller, and they went to work. They had completed an Executive Mansion and a Capitol Building and enough public buildings to accommodate most of the government offices by the time President Lamar and the Congress and fifty wagon loads of documents and archives arrived in October of the same year.

The government moved here from the city of Houston. John and Augustus Allen had persuaded the government to move to Houston shortly after they founded that city in 1836. Naming their new town for the new president of the new republic was part of their lobbying strategy, and Sam Houston apparently would have been content to have the government stay in Houston forever. It might have, if the constitution of the Republic had allowed a president to serve consecutive terms. Houston probably would have been re-elected, and he probably could have had the capital wherever he wanted it. But the constitution specified that a president could not succeed himself. Houston's term expired in December of 1838, and he was succeeded by Lamar. Lamar was supported by most of Sam Houston's critics. He and Houston disagreed about nearly everything, then and thereafter. Lamar was as anxious to move the government away from the town named for Houston as Houston was satisfied to have it there.

Houston was a member of Congress while Lamar was president, and Houston complained loudly about the re-location of the government. He claimed that Austin was 35 miles beyond the frontier and too dangerous a place to be the seat of the government. There was some truth to this. Two of

Austin was occupied by Union troops after the end of the Civil War. The commanding general had his headquarters in a stone building that had been the State Asylum for the Blind earlier. The building has been used for a number of purposes since the Union troops left. It now belongs to the University of Texas. It is on the southeastern edge of the campus, off Interstate 35.

the workmen building the capital city were scalped by Indians one night in 1839 as they slept. And the first county judge was scalped by Indians in 1841. But President Lamar ignored Houston's complaints. He also changed many of the policies Houston had followed. Lamar declared war on the Cherokees Houston regarded as blood brothers, and he was generally more hostile toward the Indian tribes and the Mexicans than Houston was.

The Lamar administration gets the blame for the incident at San Antonio that came to be known as the Council House Fight. Seven whites and thirty-five Comanches were killed as the Indians tried to avoid being made prisoners at what they had been led to believe was a peace parley. Lamar also sent an expedition to Santa Fe to try to establish trade and to offer the residents of New Mexico the chance to join the Republic of Texas. The members of that expedition were captured and locked up in Mexican jails for several months until they were released by President Santa Anna. The loser of the Battle of San Jacinto was back in charge of things in Mexico again by that time.

Lamar could not succeed himself either. His term ended in 1841, and Sam Houston was elected again. Houston promised in the campaign to undo most of what Lamar had done, and he included Austin in his list of things to be undone. Houston said he would give Austin back to the Indians and the buffalo if he were elected. The city had some lean times during Houston's second term. Houston had the Congress meet in Houston and then at Washington-on-the-Brazos. He made two attempts to move the government archives out of Austin, but a committee of Austin vigilantes outmaneuvered his agents both times. This contest became known as the Archive War. The government remained at Washington-on-the-

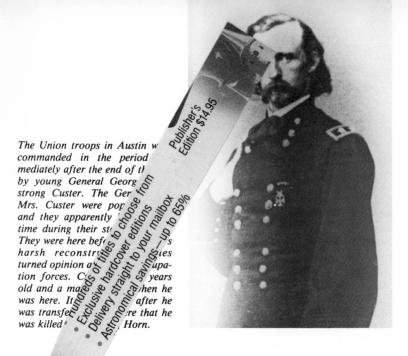

The Union troops in Austin w[...]
commanded in the period[...]
mediately after the end of th[...]
by young General Georg[...]
strong Custer. The Ger[...]
Mrs. Custer were pop[...]
and they apparently [...]
time during their st[...]
They were here bef[...]
harsh reconstr[...]ies
turned opinion a[...]upa-
tion forces. C[...]years
old and a ma[...]hen he
was here. It[...]after he
was transfe[...]re that he
was killed[...]Horn.

Braz[...] Anson Jones succeeded Houston as president. The [...]ent of the Republic never returned to Austin. But [...]e government made Austin its capital when Texas joined [...] Union in 1845. Austin has been the capital ever since. The first Texas State Legislature met in the old original log capitol building.

Sam Houston went to the United States Senate when Texas became a state. But he returned to Austin in 1859 as governor. Austin was secure and prospering by then, but Houston's stay in the governor's mansion did not have a happy ending. He and most of the people of Travis County opposed the secession the majority of Texans favored. Houston refused to take an oath of loyalty to the Confederacy. The Legislature declared the governor's office vacant and moved Lieutenant Governor Edward Clark up to replace Houston. Texas left the Union in March of 1861 and the Houstons quietly left the governor's mansion and moved to Huntsville where Sam died in 1863, two years before the Confederacy expired.

Austin was occupied by the Union Army after the end of the Civil War. A former congressman and Union sympathizer named Andrew J. Hamilton was appointed provisional governor by President Andrew Johnson when Confederate sympathizer Pendleton Murrah abandoned the governor's office and fled to Mexico. The Union troops in Austin were com-

1

2

1) The oldest government building still standing in Austin is the Governor's Mansion at 1010 Colorado, at 11th. The mansion was built in 1855 by the master builder Abner Cook. Elisha M. Pease was governor at the time. He chose the site and he was the first governor to live in the mansion. The mansion is open to the public at certain times. There is no charge. The schedule of visiting hours can be obtained by phoning 475-2121.

2) The second Texas capitol was the first capitol building on the present capitol grounds. It was a modest affair of three stories. The government remained in this building from 1853 until it burned in 1881. The Secession Convention met here in 1861 to move Texas out of the Union and into the Confederacy.

manded for a time by the flashy young General George Armstrong Custer. This was during the early days of the occupation before the Reconstruction turned ugly, and many Austin people had always sympathized with the North, anyway. So General and Mrs. Custer apparently were received kindly. They had a pleasant tour of duty here before Custer was transferred to the duty that eventually led him to Little Big Horn. The building the Custers occupied while they were in Austin is still standing.

The original plan of the city of Austin was fourteen blocks square. The streets running north and south were named for the rivers of Texas. Most of the streets running east and west were named for native trees, but these names were later changed to numbers. Live Oak Street became Second Street, Cypress became Third. Sixth Street was originally named Pecan and there is a move now to change the name back to Pecan.

The original plan set aside the four square blocks bounded by Mesquite (11th) and Peach (13th) and by Brazos and Colorado for the Capitol. The capitol property was later expanded, and the present Capitol stands on the site the original planners intended. But the first log capitol building was built three blocks to the south, at Colorado and Eighth.

The original President's House was built on the site

1) There was a showdown between two governors here in the 1853 Capitol. It happened in 1874. One of the principals was Edmund J. Davis. He was a Republican and Union sympathizer. He was elected governor in 1870 with the support of Washington and the carpetbaggers. He failed to win reelection in the fall of 1873.

2) Democrat Richard Coke got almost twice as many votes as Davis. But Davis refused to leave the governor's office when his term expired in January of 1874. He said the election was unconstitutional. The deadlock continued for several days until President Grant notified Davis there would be no U.S. intervention to keep him in power. Coke took over the office then and many Texans counted this the end of the Reconstruction Era in Texas.

bounded by Brazos, Seventh, San Jacinto and Eighth streets. The official mansion was two stories. It was built of pine from Bastrop and it was painted white. President Lamar occupied it until 1841. Houston abandoned it when he abandoned Austin and it never served as a presidential residence again. It burned in 1847. St. Mary's Academy occupied the site for a number of years. It is now a parking lot.

The present governor's mansion was built in 1856. The site at Eleventh and Colorado was chosen by Governor E. M. Pease. He was the first governor to live in the present mansion.

The present capitol building is the fourth Austin building to serve as the Texas Capitol. The original log building served until 1853. The government moved then to a new building on the present capitol grounds. The city of Austin acquired the original capitol site and built a city hall on it.

The second capitol building was three stories tall. It was built of stone, and it had a modest cupola on top. The Secession Convention met in 1861 in the second capitol building. The Constitutional Conventions of 1866 and 1868-69 met there, and so did the 1875 convention that wrote the present constitution. The second capitol building was also the scene of the showdown between the carpetbaggers' Republican governor E. J. Davis and Democrat Richard Coke.

The present State Capitol is the fourth capitol building to be built in Austin. The building was patterned after the national capitol in Washington and laid out in the form of a Greek cross. The rotunda in the center is open all the way up to the dome. There is free parking for tourists in a small lot across from the Capitol at Congress and 11th Street.

Edmund Jackson Davis was a district judge in the Rio Grande Valley when the Civil War began. He was a Union sympathizer, and he left Texas to serve in the Union Army. Davis rose to brigadier general's rank. He returned to Texas and politics when the war ended. He was chosen governor in a special election arranged by the commander of the occupation forces, and he ran the state government with almost dictatorial powers until 1873. Davis ran for re-election that year. Richard Coke beat him by a wide margin. Coke had been a captain in the Confederate Army. Coke's election marked the end of the carpetbag era in Texas, but Davis was slow to realize it. He claimed the election Coke won was unconstitutional, and he refused to give up the office. Coke and the new legislature were doing business on the second floor of the capitol building for several days while Davis and the old legislature held out on the first floor, protected by troops. Davis appealed to President U. S. Grant to save his office for him. Grant refused to intervene, and Davis finally gave up the office.

Davis continued to be a leader in Republican politics for a number of years. He enjoyed a reputation for integrity and refinement. He was buried in the State Cemetery at Austin when he died in 1883.

1

2

3

4

1) The state cut some corners in building the present Capitol. Convicts were put to work to help the contractor cut and haul the granite from Burnet County and the contractor was paid in land.

2) The building cost the contractor more than 3 million dollars and he got a little less than 1 acre of land for each dollar.

3) Senator Temple Houston made the speech when the Capitol was dedicated on May 18, 1888. He was Sam Houston's youngest son. Texas did not get clear title to the land the Capitol sits on until 1925. It was part of a grant Thomas Jefferson Chambers had obtained from the Mexican government. The state had to make a settlement with Chambers' heirs.

4) The Capitol is open to visitors and there are tours. Visitors to the chamber of the House of Representatives can see the battle flag Texans carried at San Jacinto. The flag hangs behind the Speaker's podium.

The second Texas capitol building was destroyed by fire in 1881. The legislature had started planning a majestic permanent capitol building before that time, but it was still in the planning stages. So the government of Texas had to conduct its business for several years in a temporary building put up in 1882 at the corner of Eleventh and Congress, opposite the capitol grounds. That building was the capitol until the permanent building was completed. The temporary building burned in 1899, and the site it stood on is now a small park.

1

2

1) The writer O. Henry lived and worked in Austin. His house is now a museum, open weekdays and Sunday afternoons, at 409 East 5th Street.
2) One of the places O. Henry worked here was the Old Land Office Building. This building on the Capitol grounds is now a museum, open daily except Sundays and Mondays.

Work on the present capitol building started in 1882, and the building was finished in 1888. It is the biggest state capitol building in the country. The Capitol is 566 feet long and 289 feet wide. It has 400 rooms and 18 acres of floor space. The handsome terrazzo floors were added during the Centennial observance in 1936. The state financed the construction of the Capitol by trading three million acres of state land in the Panhandle to the contractor offering the best bid. The contracting firm turned the land into the XIT Ranch and eventually recovered substantially more money than it put out in building the Capitol.

The original plan was to build the Capitol of limestone from a quarry in Travis County. But the contractors decided after the work started that the limestone was too soft and too likely to discolor. The builders and Governor John Ireland settled on Burnet County red granite, instead. This meant greater costs because the material had to be hauled a greater distance. So there were several compromises. A few porticoes were trimmed from the plans. The owners of Granite Mountain at Marble Falls donated the stone. The state built a railroad from the quarry to the capitol grounds and furnished convicts to help handle the stone. The granite cutters' union got upset about this and refused to furnish cutters for the job. The contractors imported granite cutters from Scotland, and eventually had to pay a small fine for that violation of the Federal Alien Contract Labor Law. But they got the job done. Texas accepted the capitol building on May 18, 1888 at a ceremony featuring a speech by Sam Houston's son, Senator Temple Houston.

1) The University of Texas at Austin is the biggest university in the South but hardly the oldest. Classes began in 1883.
2) The University was enriched by the discovery of oil on University lands. The rig from the original University well is displayed on the campus.

The oldest building in the capitol complex is the Governor's Mansion. The second oldest is the Old Land Office Building. This building was designed by a German architect to resemble a German castle. It was built in 1857 on the southeast corner of the capitol grounds at Eleventh and Brazos. The Land Office outgrew the old building years ago, and it has been a museum since 1919. The museum is maintained by the Daughters of the Confederacy and the Daughters of the Republic of Texas. William Sydney Porter worked for the Land Office in this building between 1887 and 1891. Porter wrote short stories under the name of O. Henry. He also published a magazine called "The Rolling Stone" during part of the time he was working in the Land Office Building. Porter married Athol Estes in Austin and lived for a while in a cottage at 308 E. 4th Street. The cottage was moved later to 409 E. 5th Street, and it is now a museum.

Porter worked for the First National Bank of Austin for three years after he left the Land Office job. He was blamed for the disappearance of some of the bank's money, and he served a short term in prison. He achieved most of his success as a writer after that.

Education was an expressed concern of the founders of Texas. The Declaration of Independence listed Mexico's failure to see to the education of its citizens as one of the settlers' grievances. So the planners of the capital city set aside a site for a university in the very beginning in 1839. But

1) Papers the late President Lyndon Johnson accumulated during his years in public life are preserved in the Lyndon Baines Johnson Library on the western edge of the U.T. campus. The library is open every day.
2) A rare Gutenberg Bible is one of the treasures on display at the U.T. Humanities Research Center. The Bible is in the Michener Gallery on the ground floor of the Research Center.

2

it was not until 1882 that work started on the first building on that 40 acres the founders named College Hill. Today, the University of Texas at Austin has more than 40,000 students attending classes on a campus that substantially exceeds 40 acres.

Some of the other institutions of higher learning in the capital city are the Austin Presbyterian Theological Seminary, Concordia Lutheran College, Episcopal Theological Seminary of the Southwest, Huston-Tillotson College and St. Edward's University.

1) Symphony Square is a little park around the old Jeremiah Hamilton Building at Red River and 11th Street. The park includes an outdoor theater.
2) The Texas Historical Commission has offices in a house Leonidas Carrington built at 1511 Colorado in 1856.
3) The old Gethsemane Church building is on the same block and it houses some of the Historical Commission offices. This building was built by Swedish Lutherans in 1883.

2

3

There are more historical markers in Travis County than in any other county in Texas. This is mostly because so much history has happened in the area and partly because the people here are very conscious of history. The state markers are made at a foundry in San Antonio, but they are approved and authorized by the Texas Historical Commission. The Commission has its offices in an old building on Colorado Street. It authorizes markers for sites and buildings after county historical commissions certify they have historic significance. No major changes can be made to the exteriors of buildings

1

1) An entire block of residential buildings in downtown Austin is listed in the National Register of Historic Places. *This is the Bremond block on Guadalupe between 7th and 8th. These houses were built in the middle to late 1800s, mostly by members of the same prosperous family. This one is occupied now by the Texas Classroom Teachers' Association. Several other organizations have offices in other buildings in the block.*

2) The cottage and the mansion Henry Hirschfield built on West 9th Street are being crowded now by commercial developments and skyscrapers, but they are protected state and national landmarks. Hirschfield built the limestone cottage first, in 1876.

3) The cottage and this mansion Hirschfield built next door in 1886 have been carefully restored. Hirschfield was a merchant and banker.

2

3

1

2

1) The house the French envoy to the Republic of Texas built at 802 San Marcos may be the oldest house still standing in Austin. Alphonse Dubois de Saligny built it in 1840. It is known as the French Legation and it is open to visitors daily except Monday. There is an admission fee. Saligny was regarded as something of a joke after he got into a spat with an Austin hotelkeeper over the behavior of the hotel man's pigs, but the letters he wrote to Paris about Texas affairs were fairly perceptive.

2) Rancher Jesse Lincoln Driskill built the Driskill Hotel at Brazos and East 7th Street in 1886 and the hotel has played an important role in Austin affairs ever since. White House press briefings were held here when Lyndon Johnson was President. Braniff International bought the Driskill in the middle 1970s and restored it.

3) The mansion pioneer rancher and banker George Littlefield built at Whitis Avenue and 24th Street in 1894 is now owned by the University of Texas.

3

awarded these markers, and there are some tax advantages for the owners. But the presence of a state marker or medallion on a home or building does not necessarily mean that it is open to the public.

The Texas Historical Commission publishes a guide to buildings and sites displaying historical markers. The commission's guide does not spell out what the notices on the markers say. But Lone Star Legends of Odessa (Box 1646, Odessa 79760) publishes a catalog of the historical markers on all the main roads in the state. This book is entitled *Why*

1) The Laguna Gloria Art Museum is the former home of the late Clara Driscoll. She was the saviour of the Alamo. She put up her own money to buy the Alamo barracks building to keep it from being torn down, and then persuaded the state to take over the whole property and turn it into a shrine. The Laguna Gloria Museum at Lake Austin is open daily except Mondays.

2) The Neill Cochran house was built at 2310 San Gabriel in about 1853 by Abner Cook. The National Society of Colonial Dames of America in Texas owns this house now and it is open to visitors from 1 p.m. to 4 p.m. Wednesdays through Sundays. There is an admission fee.

1

Stop? It does tell what is on each one of the markers listed.

A number of the buildings displaying state historical markers in Austin are also listed in the *National Register of Historic Places.* Some of these are: the homes in the Bremond block, on Guadalupe between 7th and 8th, built mostly by members of the same prosperous family; the Brizendine house built in 1873 at 507 W. 11th Street; the Carrington-Covert house built in 1857 at 1511 Colorado; the Caswell houses built in the early 1900s at 1404 and 1502 West Avenue; the Driskill Hotel built in 1886 at 117 East 7th Street; the French Legation built in 1841 at 802 San Marcos by French envoy Alphonse de Saligny; the Governor's Mansion at 1010 Colorado; the Henry Hirschfield house and cottage built in 1876 and 1886 at 303 and 305 West 9th Street; Laguna Gloria, built in 1916 at 3890 West 35th Street; the Old Land Office Building built in 1857 at 108 East 11th Street; the Littlefield house built in 1894 at 24th and Whitis; the Neill-Cochran house built in 1853 at 2310 San Gabriel; the Elisabet Ney Studio built in 1893 at 304 East 44th Street; and the

1

2

1) *The home where the sculptor Elisabet Ney lived and worked is a museum now. The Ney place is at 304 East 44th Street. The exhibits include some contemporary art and a collection of Elisabet Ney's sculpture. She was a successful sculptor in Europe before she and her husband moved to Texas in 1872. She did the statues of Sam Houston and Stephen F. Austin for the Capitol. People in Austin thought Elisabet Ney was a little strange because she used her maiden name and lived and worked in Austin while her husband lived at their plantation.*

2) *St. Mary's Cathedral was designed by the Galveston architect Nicholas Clayton. It was built in 1874 at 201 East 10th Street. The cathedral is listed in the* National Register of Historic Places.

3) *Austin's gifted Abner Cook built the mansion known as "Woodlawn" at Niles Road and Pease in 1853. The late Governor E. M. Pease and his descendants owned this house from 1857 until 1957. Former Governor and Mrs. Allan Shivers live here, now. The house is not open to the public.*

3

3

1) *The Texas Declaration of Independence and other historic documents are on display in the Lorenzo de Zavala State Archives and Library Building at 1201 Brazos, adjacent to the Capitol. The library is open all day, weekdays.*
2) *Sam Houston is buried at Huntsville, but many of the other great names of Texas history are chiseled on monuments in the State Cemetery on Comal at East 7th, in Austin.*
3) *One of the markers in the State Cemetery appears to suggest that Susana Dickinson is buried in the official cemetery, but her grave is actually in Section 1 of the Oakwood Cemetery where this marker is. Susana Dickinson was a survivor of the Siege of the Alamo. She was Mrs. Almaron Dickinson. She and her infant daughter were in the old mission on March 6th, 1836, when Santa Anna's troops swarmed in and killed Almaron Dickinson and all the other defenders. Santa Anna gave Mrs. Dickinson and her baby an escort to Gonzales where the rest of the Texas Army was camped at the time. She later married John Hannig and lived with him in Austin until she died in 1883. Her grave is in the Hannig family plot in Oakwood.*

1   2

3

1) Zilker Park is a beauty spot surrounding the popular Barton Springs swimming resort on the south side of the Colorado. The pool here is fed by natural springs. The temperature remains at 68 degrees the year around. The springs took their name from William Barton. He settled on this attractive spot in 1837, two years before Mirabeau Lamar conceived the idea of building a city here. You may see women bathers here without tops. It will do no good to complain. Tops are optional.

2) One of the factors contributing to Austin's fame as an uncommonly pleasant place to live is the abundance of parks in appropriate places like the one on top of Mount Bonnell that provides this view of Lake Austin in one direction and a view of the city in the other direction. The road to the top of Mount Bonnell begins at the west end of West 35th Street.

3) The first real dam in Texas was about where the present Tom Miller Dam impounding Lake Austin is today. The original dam broke during a flood in 1900. A second dam here washed away, too, before the Lower Colorado River Authority built the Tom Miller Dam in 1940.

"Woodlawn" mansion built in 1853 by Austin's master builder Abner Cook, at 6 Niles Road. "Woodlawn" was owned for a hundred years by former Governor E. M. Pease and his descendants. It is owned now by former Governor and Mrs. Allan Shivers. St. Edward's University, St. Mary's Cathedral, the Gethsemane Church and the Capitol Building also are listed in the *National Register of Historic Places*.

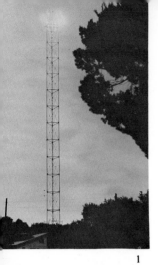

1) Austin is lighted at night by conventional street lights plus batteries of floodlights mounted on about two dozen tall towers scattered around town. Several cities once had these moonlight towers but Austin is the only city still using them. They were installed in 1895. The city got them in a trade for the railroad that it had built to haul materials for the first dam on the Colorado River in 1893.

2) Austin has been the county seat of Travis County since the county was organized in 1840. The present courthouse at Guadalupe and 10th was built in 1930.

3) A rock house Charles Johnson built on the bank of the Colorado in 1858 has since become the headquarters of the Travis Post 76 of the American Legion. And the Colorado has become Town Lake at this point. The Johnson house is at West 1st Street and the MoPac Expressway.

1

2

3

Travis County was formed in 1840 from part of the original Bastrop County after the city of Austin was established. The county was named for the Alamo hero. The city of Austin has been the county seat from the beginning. The present courthouse was built in 1930.

The county has some oil and gas, stone quarries and sand and gravel. There is some farming and ranching, but education, government and recreation are the biggest factors in the economy of Travis County.

1

1) *A museum at Camp Mabry in the 2500 block of West 35th Street displays relics and trophies of Texas' Thirty-Sixth Division. The museum is open all day, every day. Camp Mabry was established in 1890 as a summer training ground for the Texas Volunteer Guard. Several units of the Texas National Guard, the Texas Rangers and the highway patrol have headquarters here. The base was named for Governor Jim Hogg's adjutant general W. H. Mabry because he raised most of the money that paid for the land.*

2) *Austin's other major military base is Bergstrom Air Force Base. Some of the B-52 bombers of the Strategic Air Command were based here once. But Bergstrom is now part of the Tactical Air Command, headquarters for the Twelfth Air Force, and home base for the 67th Tactical Reconnaissance Squadron. Bergstrom was named, at the suggestion of then Congressman Lyndon Johnson, for Captain John Bergstrom. He was a native of Austin, killed by a Japanese bomb in the Philippines in December of 1941. Bergstrom is on State Highway 71, south of Austin, but there are no tours and visitors are allowed only on special occasions.*

2

1

2

1) *The Old Main Building at St. Edwards University dominates the skyline on the south side of the Colorado. St. Edward's started as a boys' school. It is a co-educational university, now. Old Main was built in 1888.*

2) *Lakeway started as a resort on Lake Travis, in northwest Travis County, above Lake Austin. Lakeway is now a substantial community with many year-around homes, a golf course and a major tennis complex. Lakeway is on the western shore of the lake, off U.S. 71.*

3) *Another resort in western Travis County is Hamilton Pool, on Farm Road 3238, off U.S. 71. The pool is fed by a creek flowing over a limestone cliff. The late Governor A. J. Hamilton supposedly spent a lot of time at this cool retreat, contemplating his problems. Hamilton was a member of Congress and a Union sympathizer when Texas seceded in 1861. Abraham Lincoln appointed Hamilton military governor of Texas. He stayed in the north until the Civil War ended. Governor Pendleton Murrah fled to Mexico, then, and Hamilton came to Austin to take over the governor's office. His family owned the land around this pool at the time and that is how the pool got its name. The pool is still privately owned but the owner allows swimming, picnicking and camping, for a fee.*

4) *Thomas McKinney settled on this site in the 1850s. He built a grist mill and raised racehorses. McKinney's home is now a ruin. The mill is gone, but the foundations are still visible. The McKinney place is now McKinney Falls State Park, with provisions for camping and screened shelters for rent. The park is off U.S. 183, south of Austin. There is an admission fee.*

3

4

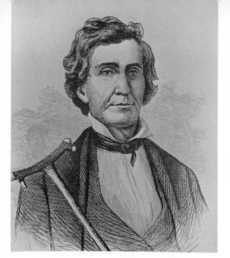

1

2

1) Williamson County was named for Robert McAlpin Williamson. He was crippled by an illness when he was a child in Georgia. But Williamson was admitted to the bar before he was 19. He came to Texas in 1826 when he was 22. He was a leader in the campaign for independence from Mexico. He fought at San Jacinto and served in the congress of the Republic. He was so much in favor of joining Texas to the United States that he named one of his sons Annexus.

2) Sam Bass' name is connected with the history of Williamson County about as firmly as Williamson's name is. Bass was one of the notorious bandits of the 1870s. Texas Rangers ambushed him here in 1878 as he was about to rob the bank that then occupied the building where Robertson's store is today.

WILLIAMSON COUNTY

Williamson County was created from part of Milam County. It was organized in 1848. The county is named for Robert McAlpin Williamson. Williamson came to Texas from Georgia in 1826. He practiced law and fought at San Jacinto. He was a member of the first Supreme Court of the Republic of Texas. He served in the Congress of the Republic and in the Legislature after Texas became a state. He was buried at Wharton when he died there in 1859, but his remains were later moved to the State Cemetery in Austin. Williamson had an illness when he was a child and it left him with a stiff right leg. His right knee was bent permanently backward. He had a wooden leg fitted at the right knee. He walked on that with his right foot dangling behind. So he was called "Three-legged Willie." It was not in derision. He was respected and popular.

Williamson County has some oil and gas and some light industry, but the main businesses are farming and ranching.

One of the older settlements is Round Rock on Interstate 35 about 18 miles north of Austin. This town is best known as

1) Sam Bass was born in Indiana in 1851. He came to Texas in 1870. He was a cowhand and a jockey before he started robbing banks. This is believed to be a picture of Bass as a young man, but there is some uncertainty about it.
2) Bass died two days after he was shot in the ambush at Round Rock. He was buried here at the edge of the old Round Rock slave cemetery on what has ever since been known as Sam Bass Road. He was no Robin Hood, but he became a hero in cowboy ballads after the rangers killed him.

the place where the outlaw Sam Bass made his last stand. Bass and his gang made a business of robbing trains and stagecoaches in Nebraska and Texas in the 1870s. They came to Round Rock in July of 1878 to rob the bank. But one of Sam's cronies tipped off the Texas Rangers. The rangers ambushed the Bass Gang here on July 19th. The robbery was thwarted, and Bass was wounded. He died two days later, and he was buried in Round Rock. There is a dry goods store today in the building where that bank was in 1878.

The town of Round Rock was founded in 1850. It was originally called Brushy because it is on the bank of Brushy Creek. But there is a big round rock in the bed of the creek here. It has been a landmark for travelers from the time people started traveling this way. The Chisholm Trail crossed the

1) The settlement now called Round Rock was established in 1850 on the bank of Brushy Creek. The settlement was called Brushy at first. But the landmark all travelers knew best was a big round rock at the creek crossing. So the settlement gradually came to be called Round Rock instead of Brushy. The trail used by the stagecoaches and cattle drivers crossed the creek here.

2) The Round Rock newspaper was established in 1875. The Leader was one of the last weekly papers in the state to give up setting type by hand. That was in 1972. The paper has a modern plant, now.

creek at the round rock. So the town on the creek at the round rock eventually came to be called Round Rock.

The oldest part of Round Rock is on the west side of I-35. Most of the commercial interests moved eastward to be closer to the railroad when it came through. The old stagecoach inn, in the old section, at FM 620 and Limestone Road, is now a private home. The site where the Trinity Lutheran College stood from 1904 to 1930 is now the Trinity Lutheran Home for the Aged. The "Round Rock Leader" founded in 1875, is still being published here.

An old ranch house built in the 1840s has been converted to a restaurant. It is called the Inn at Brushy Creek, and it is just west of I-35 at the U.S. 79 exit.

A marker on U.S. 79, about two and a half miles east of Round Rock, recalls some of the history of Kenney's Fort. Dr. Thomas Kenney established a little stockaded village here in 1838 or 1839. It was about the first settlement in what is now Williamson County. President Lamar launched his Santa

27

1

2

3

1) Captain Nelson Merrell built this home in 1870. It is on U.S. 79 east of Interstate 35 and it is listed in the National Register of Historic Places.
2) The Woodbine Mansion on Main Street in Round Rock was built in 1895. It and the Merrell house are private residences.
3) Dr. Thomas Kenney established a little settlement east of Round Rock in 1839. It was one of the earliest settlements in Williamson County.

Fe Expedition from Kenney's Fort in 1841. And it was at Kenney's Fort that vigilantes from Austin overtook and overpowered Sam Houston's agents in 1843, on one of the occasions when they tried to move the Texas archives away from

1) *A marker in the Davis Cemetery near Leander recalls that about 30 settlers were killed here when Indians ambushed a wagon train in 1839. The city of Austin had just been established at the time and this part of Texas was Comanche country.*

2) *The late Governor Dan Moody Jr. was born in Taylor. His father was mayor of the town.*

3) *The old Moody home in Taylor is now a museum. The museum is open Saturday and Sunday afternoons and by appointment. The address is 144 West 9th Street in Taylor.*

Austin. Dr. Kenney was killed by Comanches in 1844. There is nothing left of his fort.

Another encounter between Indians and settlers is commemorated by markers at Leander in southwestern Williamson County. The markers say about thirty settlers were traveling westward through here in the summer of 1839 in a wagon train led by John Webster. Comanches ambushed the party and killed all but three. The victims were buried in a single grave in what is now known as Davis Cemetery, on FM 2243, a mile and a half east of Leander. A marker on U.S. 183 near the intersection of FM 2243 points to the site of the Webster massacre.

The biggest town in Williamson County is Taylor, on State Highway 79, east of Round Rock. Taylor is not quite as old as some of the other cities in Williamson County. It was born with the railroad era in 1876 and named for a railroad man.

The first mayor of Taylor was Daniel Moody. Mayor

1

2

3

1) The city of Georgetown is the county seat of Williamson County. There was no city here when the county was organized in 1848. George Glasscock owned the land where the city is. He donated the land for the townsite. The present courthouse was built in 1910.

2) The Dimmitt Building at 801 Main Street is one of the Georgetown buildings awarded an historical marker. John Jones Dimmitt built it. He was a pioneer surveyor, lawyer and railroad promoter. He is credited with helping get Southwestern University moved to Georgetown.

3) Southwestern University opened in Georgetown in 1873 as Texas University. The name was changed to Southwestern in 1875. Several early Methodist schools were merged to create this one. One of the forerunners dated from 1840, so Southwestern claims it is the oldest Texas institution of higher education in continuous operation. The ornate administration building is listed in the National Register of Historic Places. *It was completed in 1900.*

Moody's son went into politics, too. Dan Jr. was governor of Texas from 1927 to 1931. The Moody home is now a museum. It is open on Saturday and Sunday afternoons and other times by appointment. The location is 144 W. 9th Street in Taylor. The father of another governor spent some time in this area, too. Captain Shapley Ross commanded a company

1

2

1) There are several attractive swimming holes along the San Gabriel River in Georgetown. This one is Blue Hole near the San Gabriel Park. The park is an old Indian campground.
2) A new lake forming behind a new dam on the North San Gabriel will expand the recreational opportunities considerably. It is called Lake Georgetown.
3) The Sherman Lesene family makes candles in a factory on Interstate 35 in Georgetown. The Mar-Jon Candle Factory operates seven days a week and visitors are welcome every day.

3

of rangers stationed on the San Gabriel River near where Georgetown is today. That was in 1846. The captain was the father of Lawrence "Sul" Ross. Sul was a ranger, too, before he was elected governor in 1887.

The city of Georgetown on I-35 about 28 miles north of Austin is the county seat of Williamson County. The city was founded at about the same time the county was organized in 1848, at the junction of the North and South San Gabriel Rivers. The present courthouse was built in 1910.

One of the founders of this city was George Washington Glasscock. He donated the land for the townsite and the settlement was named Georgetown in his honor. Glasscock came to Texas in 1834. He had been in partnership briefly before that with Abraham Lincoln in a riverbarge business in Illinois.

Georgetown is the home of Southwestern University. This school resulted from the merger of the Rutersville College, Wesleyan College, McKenzie College and Soule University in 1873. The combined Methodist school opened its doors to male students that year as Texas University. The name was ›

Workmen building the Interstate Highway here in the 1960s discovered a limestone cavern beside the highway right of way. The cave is now called Inner Space Cavern. It is just off Interstate 35 south of Georgetown. There is an admission fee.

changed to Southwestern in 1875 and women students were admitted for the first time in 1878.

There is a limestone cave just south of Georgetown on I-35 called the Inner Space Cavern. It is open to visitors every day during the summer months and every day except Monday and Tuesday during the winter. Fees are $5 for adults and $2.50 for children. There are tours every 20 minutes. This cavern is ancient, but nobody knew about it until 1963. Workmen discovered it when they were punching holes in the ground in preparation for the building of I-35.

The Mar-Jon Candle Factory on I-35 in Georgetown claims to produce a wider assortment of candles than any other candle concern in the state. The Mar-Jon Factory is operated by members of the Sherman Lesesne family, and they welcome visitors to the place seven days a week.

Some of the buildings in Georgetown with historical markers are the Shafer Saddle Shop at 711 Main, the Dimmitt Building at 801 Main, the Dimmitt home on State Highway 29 at the edge of town, the Southwestern University Main Building at 1000 East University (State Highway 29), and the G. W. Riley home at 1302 College.

A family named Beck has developed a western clothing store and barbecue restaurant in an old cotton gin at Florence. Florence is on State Highway 195 in northwestern Williamson County, on the road to Burnet County.

1

1) There is a museum now at the site where the U.S. Army in 1849 built the fort that was to protect this part of the frontier. The Burnet County Historical Society has restored an old stone powder house that was part of the fort. Four other old buildings have been moved to the site and a number of other relics of the frontier days are on display at the Fort Croghan Museum on State Highway 29, west of Burnet. The museum is open weekdays during the summer and there is a small admission fee.

2) Burnet County was named for David G. Burnet. He was acting president of Texas during the revolution and he signed the Treaties of Velasco with President Santa Anna after Sam Houston's army captured Santa Anna at San Jacinto. Burnet is pronounced "burn-it."

2

BURNET COUNTY

This county is named for the first chief executive of the Republic of Texas. David Gouverneur Burnet was born in New Jersey in 1788. He came to Texas the first time in about 1815 and he came to stay in 1826. He obtained authority from the Mexican government to settle immigrants in southeast Texas, and he was one of the early advocates of separation from Mexico. Burnet was named interim president by the Convention of 1836 that wrote the Texas Declaration of Independence at Washington-on-the-Brazos. Burnet served until the fall of 1836, when Sam Houston was elected president. Burnet later served as vice president and acting president during M. B. Lamar's administration. He died in Galveston in 1870. He is buried in the State Cemetery.

Burnet County was created in 1852 from parts of Williamson, Travis and Bell counties. A few settlers came into the

1

2

3

1) The town of Burnet was originally called Hamilton Valley. It has been the county seat since Burnet County was organized in 1854. The present courthouse was built in 1936.

2) The Whitaker house at 802 South Main was built in 1870. It is a private residence.

3) A colony of Mormons settled on Hamilton Creek in 1845. The Mormons built a mill on the creek about 8 miles south of the present town of Burnet. They stayed only a short time but other owners continued to operate the mill until 1901. Little is left at the site now except the creek itself.

area before that. The first permanent settler was Samuel Eley Holland. He came to Texas from Georgia in 1848. The rangers had a small camp at the time on Hamilton Creek about three miles south of the present town of Burnet. The little ranger station was commanded by Henry E. McCulloch, and it was called Camp McCulloch. U.S. troops replaced the rangers at the camp in March of 1849.

The federal troops changed the location of the camp a few months later and developed a frontier outpost that eventually was named Fort Croghan. The fort was abandoned after the frontier moved farther west in 1855. Some of the buildings became private homes, and some fell down. But some of them have been rebuilt now, and they are part of a museum at the site of the fort on State Highway 29, west of Burnet.

A little settlement that grew up near the fort on Hamilton Creek was known in the beginning as Hamilton Valley. This settlement became the county seat when Burnet County was established, and it took the same name as the county. The present courthouse in Burnet was built in 1936.

Historic buildings in Burnet include the old Cook house at 200 North Main Street and the old Whitaker house at 802

1

2

1) The Longhorn Cavern in Longhorn Cavern State Park is one of the world's larger caves. The park is on Park Road 4 in western Burnet County. There are no provisions for camping in this park, but campsites are available at Inks Lake State Park on State Highway 29, 9 miles west of Burnet.
2) There was a night club with a dance floor in Longhorn Cavern for a time during the 30s before it became a park. The place has natural air conditioning. Indians lived here years ago. Bandits hid out here in the frontier days and there was a Confederate gunpowder plant here during the Civil War.

South Main Street. Both are private residences.

Elder Lyman Wight brought a band of Mormons into Texas in 1845. They settled first in Grayson County and then tried a couple of other locations before they moved to this area in 1851. The Mormons set up a grist mill and a furniture factory on Hamilton Creek. They stayed only a couple of years and then sold out to a man named Noah Smithwick and moved on. Smithwick had been an armorer at Fort Croghan and he apparently had another grist mill or two. He was also the author of *Evolution of a State.* Smithwick was opposed to secession, so he sold his mills and moved to California in 1861. The mill on Hamilton Creek continued to operate under other owners until about 1901. Ruins of the settlement and the mill are still visible about 8 miles south of Burnet by way of South Pierce Street and Mormon Mill Road.

The Longhorn Cavern State Park is southwest of Burnet, about 11 miles. Access is by Park Road 4, off U.S. 281. The park is open every day between March and October and every day except Mondays and Tuesdays between October and March. Tours of the cavern are $3 each for adults and $2 each for children between 6 and 12. Children under 6 get in free if they are with adults, and there are special prices for groups and students. You can get more information from the park manager, Park Road 4, Route 2, Burnet, Texas 78611.

There are no provisions for camping overnight in the Longhorn Cavern State Park. But Park Road 4 leads on west and north to a park that does have provisions for camping.

1) Burnet County has frontage on five of the Highland Lakes, and some fine scenery. A lookout point on Farm Road 1431 provides this view of the junction of the Colorado River and the Llano at the upper end of Lake Lyndon B. Johnson. This lake is one of the projects of the Lower Colorado River Authority. It was originally called Granite Shoals Lake.

This is the Inks Lake State Park at Inks Lake. It is one of the state's Class I parks. There is the usual admission fee of $2 per vehicle unless you have the annual permit you can obtain for $15 from the Texas Department of Parks and Wildlife, or the Senior Citizens' Passport you can obtain from the same place for nothing if you are over 65.

There are additional charges for campsites and shelters. The Inks Lake Park has 197 campsites and 22 screened shelters. The address for reservations is Box 117, Buchanan Dam, Texas 78609.

Inks Lake was built in 1938 by the Lower Colorado River Authority to control flooding on the Colorado and to furnish power for electric generating plants. Lake Buchanan, above Inks Lake, and Lake Lyndon B. Johnson and Lake Marble Falls, below Inks Lake, are part of the same L.C.R.A. project. The Colorado River and these lakes form the western boundary of Burnet County. The river turns east across the southern end of the county and flows into Lake Travis. The northern end of Lake Travis forms part of the southeastern boundary of the county. So Burnet County has frontage on five major lakes. The combination of the hills, the river and the lakes makes for some picturesque scenery.

Burnet County Park is a popular fishing spot on the east shore of Lake Buchanan. Take Ranch Road 2341 north from State Highway 29 to get there.

Marble Falls got its name from some outcroppings of marble in the bed of the Colorado. But this area has more granite

*1) There is a little marble at Marble Falls in southern Burnet County. But
there is a lot more granite. The Granite Mountain Quarry, half a mile west of
Marble Falls on Farm Road 1431, furnished the stone for the State Capitol
and for the seawall at Galveston and there is plenty of granite here still.
2) The passenger trains are only a dim memory in this part of Texas, but an
old passenger depot lives on in Marble Falls as the office of the Chamber of
Commerce.*

than marble. All the granite for the State Capitol Building
and for the Galveston Seawall, too, came from Granite
Mountain, half a mile west of Marble Falls off Ranch Road
1431. The quarry here has furnished stone for numerous
other major projects, but it is far from exhausted. There is
more rock left in the giant granite dome than has been hauled
away. The quarry is older than the town of Marble Falls.
Quarrying began at Granite Mountain in the early 1880s. The
town of Marble Falls was not founded by Adam R. Johnson
until 1887. Johnson was a vigorous promoter of water power
and Marble Falls. But he never saw his town. He was a
general in the Confederate cavalry during the Civil War, and
he was blinded in a battle in Kentucky, 23 years before he
founded Marble Falls.

Oscar Fox could see what Adam Johnson could not, and
Fox composed a song about it. A marker in the roadside park
on U.S. 281, just south of Marble Falls, reminds us that this is
the scenery Fox praised in his song *The Hills of Home.*

The stone outcroppings here in Burnet County are part of
what is called the Llano Uplift. Feldspar, garnet, quartz and
topaz are found here in addition to the marble and granite
already mentioned. There is a major graphite mine near
Burnet. Rockhounds should check with landowners, of
course, before they do any prospecting, and they should not
do any prospecting in state parks.

There is more information about rocks in *Texas Rocks and
Minerals, Guidebook 6,* published by the Bureau of

1) *Mineral springs drew people to the spot that is now the city of Lampasas. Elaborate bathhouses were built in the 1880s here at Hancock Springs on Sulphur Creek. There was a fancy hotel at Hancock Springs during the days of the railroad boom when people all over America were flocking to spas. The area is now a city park. The springs are still flowing.*

2) *The hotel at Hancock Springs burned to the ground one cold night in February of 1895. But the old Keystone Hotel is still standing on 2nd Street in Lampasas. The Keystone was built in 1870. It was restored in 1978 to house the Lampasas Savings and Loan Association.*

2

Economic Geology, University of Texas, Box X, University Station, Austin, Texas 78712 (at $1.81), and in *Gem Trails of Texas,* published by Gem Trails Publishing Company, Box 157, Glen Rose, Texas 76043 (at $4.20).

LAMPASAS COUNTY

This county is named for the Lampasas River, and the river's name is a mistake. The water in the Lampasas is slightly salty. It is generally believed that the early Spanish explorers named the stream Salado, because of the saltiness. The theory is that the same early explorers gave the name Lampasas to a stream in what is now Bell County. Lampasas is Spanish for lillies. But some mapmaker along the way transposed the two names. The salty stream got named for the lillies and became the Lampasas. The stream with the lillies got the name intended for the salty stream and became Salado Creek.

The county's western boundary is the Colorado River, and

1) The settlement that became Lampasas was originally called Burleson because the first landowner was named John Burleson. The name was changed to Lampasas Springs in 1856 when the county was formed. Lampasas Springs was eventually shortened to Lampasas. The present courthouse is the third one the county has built.
2) The old Lampasas stagecoach inn is now a private residence. This building is at 511 South Western. It was built in 1856.

it was water that drew the first people here. There are springs here charged with sulphur and iron salts. The Indians thought the water was healthful, and they had a campground where the city of Lampasas is today. The first white settlers came because of the reputed medicinal value of the spring water. Those first whites came about 1853. This area was the frontier at that time, and the original settlers endured additional hardships because a drought in 1855 and 1856 ruined their crops. Some of the springs that were the original attraction are still flowing mineral water, in Hancock Park, about half a mile from the present courthouse.

Lampasas County was organized in 1856 from parts of Travis and Bell counties. The little settlement at the springs was known until then as Burleson. The name was changed to Lampasas when the settlement became the county seat. The present courthouse in Lampasas was designed by W. C. Dodson and built in 1883 of native limestone.

The original Texas Chapter of the Farmers' Alliance was established in a country schoolhouse on Donaldson Creek here in Lampasas County in 1877. The alliance was intended to protect farmers from land speculators and to improve economic conditions. The original Farmers' Alliance was later reorganized and then merged with the Farmers' Union of Louisiana and that group eventually became part of the Farmers' Alliance and Co-Operative Union of America.

There is more ranching than farming in Lampasas County today. The first railroad reached here in 1882.

Major John B. Jones of the Texas Rangers had to come to Lampasas in 1877 to stop a deadly feud. He made the feuding parties sign a peace treaty. Jones was the head man in the rangers at the time. He also was the master mind of the ambush that ended Sam Bass' life the following year. Jones later was Adjutant General of Texas.

One of the famous feuds of early Texas had its beginning and its end here in Lampasas County. The principals were five brothers named Horrell and their relatives and in-laws, on one side, and John Pinckney Higgins and his family on the other side. But the original incident did not involve the Higginses. The trouble started when the Horrell boys clashed with the State Police in Jerry Scott's Saloon in Lampasas. The State Police were organized by Republican Governor E. J. Davis during the meanest days of the "Reconstruction" in 1870. State Police troopers provoked about as many problems as they solved. They were given to entering homes without warrants, breaking up Democratic political gatherings, stuffing ballot boxes, and making false arrests, so it is difficult to say which party should be blamed for what happened between the Horrells and the State Police in that saloon that day in 1873. But four state police officers were dead, and Mart Horrell was wounded when the shooting stopped. Mart Horrell was arrested and taken to the jail at Georgetown. His brothers, Sam, Ben, Merritt and Tom helped him break out as soon as he recovered from his wounds, and all five Horrells then skipped out to New Mexico. They stayed there less than a year, and they apparently were involved in one scrape after another. Seventeen men, including Ben Horrell and one of the Horrells' in-laws, were killed in clashes involving the Horrell brothers in New Mexico before the surviving brothers moved back to the Lampasas area in 1874. The Horrells settled in Burnet County just outside Lampasas, and they were soon involved with their former neighbor, Higgins, in a dispute over

1

2

3

1) Lampasas has several stone houses built in the 1800s. An early settler named Moses Hughes built this one. New owners have started restoring it.

2) The house at 205 East 2nd Street in Lampasas is called the Huling Cottage, but it was built in 1860 by somebody else. Mrs. Elizabeth Huling bought it in 1872 for 3000 gold dollars.

3) The house at 402 South Broad was built by P. N. Hargraves in 1883. It became a Methodist parsonage in 1913.

livestock. Higgins claimed the Horrells were stealing his cows. There was a confrontation in Jerry Scott's Saloon in Lampasas on January 22, 1877. Higgins shot Merritt Horrell to death. The three surviving brothers vowed to get even. Two of the Horrell boys were wounded in an ambush outside town the following month, and there was a shootout on the streets of Lampasas a couple of months later. One of Higgins' in-laws was killed, and one of the Horrells' in-laws was wounded.

The Reconstruction Era in Texas ended, and the State Police were disbanded in 1875. The Texas Rangers became the principal agents of law and order again. Major John B. Jones and a party of rangers moved into the Lampasas area in the summer of 1877 to put a stop to the Horrell-Higgins feud. The rangers surprised the Horrell brothers in their beds one night and arrested them. Jones and his rangers then ordered Higgins and the Horrells to sign a treaty promising to stop shooting at each other. They signed and they apparently did no more shooting at each other. But the following year Mart

1) This marker near Lometa marks the route of the first thoroughfare through the area that is now Lampasas County. The road connecting Austin with Fort Phantom Hill at Abilene came this way. The marker is on U.S. 190 about 1 mile west of Lometa.

2) The oldest home in Lampasas County is the rock building known as the Huling Mansion. Work was started on this house in 1855. This is a private residence. It is on Farm Road 580, west of Lampasas.

and Tom Horrell were killed by a mob after they were accused of robbing and killing a country storekeeper.

Lampasas County was the birthplace and the final home of the late New York journalist Stanley Walker. He was city editor of the *New York Herald Tribune* and author of *The Night Club Era* and *Mrs. Astor's Horse.* The Walker home was near the intersection of U.S. 281 and Farm Road 1690, south of Adamsville.

Some of the buildings around Lampasas with historical markers are the Keystone Hotel on Second Street; the Huling cottage at 205 East Second; the W. N. Huling town home at 204 South Main; the Northington house at 803 South Live Oak; the Abney house at 402 South Broad; the Hart home at 511 Western Avenue; the old Huling mansion on Farm Road 580, five miles west of Lampasas; and the old Moses Hughes home on Farm Road 580, seven and a half miles west of town.

SAN SABA COUNTY

Settlement of the area that became San Saba County was an idea long before it was a reality. Henry Fisher and Burchard Miller organized the San Saba Company in 1839, and in 1842 the company obtained a grant from the Republic of Texas to settle one thousand European immigrants in this area. Fisher and Miller never brought any settlers in. They sold their interest in the grant in 1845 to the German syndicate that settled New Braunfels and Fredericksburg.

A marker on the courthouse grounds in San Saba proclaims this county as the pecan capital of the world. San Saba pecans were being exported through Galveston and Indianola as early as the 1850s. San Saba has been the county seat of San Saba County since the county was formed in 1856. The present courthouse was built in 1910.

The name of San Saba crops up in most of the legends about lost gold mines in the Texas Hill Country. There has been some prospecting in this county, and small traces of gold have been found here from time to time, but there are no gold mines. The legends of the lost San Saba mine are mostly related to the Spanish mission known as San Sabá de la Santa Cruz. The mission was established in 1757, farther up the San Saba River, near where the city of Menard is today. The Spanish may have had some kind of mine there, but the mission was abandoned after a few years, and it is doubtful that would have happened if precious metals had been found there in any quantity.

The San Saba Mission gave the San Saba River its name, and the city and county of San Saba took their names from the river. The city has been the county seat since the county was formed from part of Bexar County in 1856. The present courthouse in San Saba was built of native stone in 1910.

Ranching and farming are the main occupations here. Farmers were practicing irrigation here as early as 1860. Pecans are a major crop, and they have been from the beginning. Native San Saba pecans were being exported through Indianola and Galveston as early as the 1850s. Much of the work involved in improving pecans was done here, and San Saba's claim that it is the pecan capital is a valid one.

The German settler Hans von Meusebach negotiated a treaty with the Comanche Indians here in 1847. Meusebach took over leadership of the Adelsverein German settlement syndicate from Prince Carl of Solms-Braunfels. Prince Carl went back to Germany after he founded the settlement at New Braunfels. He left the affairs of the syndicate in some confusion.

43

1

2

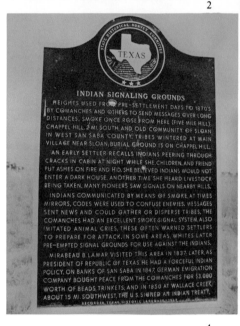

3

4

1) Hans von Meusebach gave up his German citizenship and changed his name to John Meusebach when he decided to stay in Texas. He managed some of the early settlements here after he made one of the few enduring treaties with the Indians.

2) There is a marker at the site near the present city of San Saba where Meusebach met with the chiefs of the Comanches in 1847. He offered money and fair treatment.

3) Chief Buffalo Hump and the other Comanche leaders agreed they would not bother the settlers if the settlers did not bother them. Whites often claimed the Indians never kept their promises. But the evidence suggests the Indians were as faithful to their promises as they thought the other parties were. This treaty never was violated on either side.

4) A marker on U.S. 190, 5 miles east of San Saba, recalls that the Comanches had a system of communications superior to anything the whites had in the early days. The Indians used fires on the hills here to relay smoke signals to their various camps. News of the chiefs' talks with Meusebach was sent to the other Indians this way.

San Saba is blessed with plenty of water. The town is on the San Saba River and there is a prolific spring on the eastern edge of town. There was a mill at the spring in the 1870s. The site is a city park now. The spring in Millpond Park supplies San Saba's water needs with a considerable surplus.

Meusebach apparently was more practical than the prince. He personally managed the settlement of Fredericksburg. He became a citizen of Texas and Anglicized his name to John Meusebach. And he personally sought out the chiefs of the Comanches to work out a peace agreement with them. Fredericksburg was on the frontier at the time, and this area that is now San Saba County was beyond the frontier. It was Comanche territory. The Comanches maintained signal stations on the hilltops here. They relayed intelligence and marching orders by smoke signals. This signal system kept the Comanche chiefs advised of Meusebach's progress when he and a few of his followers came here to talk about the safety of future settlers.

The Comanche chiefs Santana and Buffalo Hump and Old Owl talked with Meusebach and the settlers for two days. They agreed that the Indians would not bother Meusebach's settlers, and they agreed that the Indians would be welcome to visit the white settlements. There were provisions for the payment of money to the Comanches and provisions for settling any complaints about violations of the agreement. Other settlers elsewhere had great difficulties with the Comanches, but the German settlers had very little trouble after the Meusebach Treaty was completed. There is a marker on Farm Road 2732, sixteen miles west of San Saba, at the site where this remarkable treaty was negotiated.

San Saba has an historical museum in Mill Pond Park, five blocks east of the courthouse. Collections of early tools and equipment and furnishings are displayed in two ancient log cabins. The San Saba County Historical Museum is open regularly only on Sunday afternoons, but tours can sometimes be arranged at other times. The mailing address is

1) The First Methodist Church at 204 West Brown Street in San Saba was founded in 1856. The present building was built in 1914 and it is reputed to be the only Methodist church in the United States made entirely of marble.

2) The area around this waterfall on the Colorado has been turned into a campground. Gorman Falls Camp is on the Colorado about 5 miles below the town of Bend in southeast San Saba County. It is a popular fishing spot. The camp is privately owned. The owner charges an admission fee and there are additional charges for campsites. He also has some cabins for rent. The address for additional information is Gorman Falls Camp, General Delivery, Bend, 76824.

Route 2, Box 58, San Saba 76877. There is no admission fee.

San Saba is a small town, and the other settlements in San Saba County are much smaller. Harkeyville has disappeared from most maps. The Harkey family used to raise racehorses, and there was a noted horse track at Harkeyville. There is little left now except a marker on a country road, off U.S. 190, about three miles west of San Saba.

Skeeterville, at the north end of the county where Brushy Creek and Wilbarger Creek flow together, was so named because the most noticeable thing about the site was the abundance of mosquitoes.

This part of the Hill Country is popular with hunters. White-tailed deer are especially plentiful here. The hunting is mostly on private property by arrangement with the property owners. Hunters must have state licenses, obtainable at the county courthouses and at most sporting goods stores. Information about seasons and the bag and possession limits can be obtained from the Department of Parks and Wildlife, 4200 Smith School Road, Austin 78744, or by calling the department's toll-free information number, 1-800-252-9327.

Texas has never had a gold boom. But if there ever is a gold boom in the state it may be here. Some geologists say the place gold is most likely to be found in Texas is along Sandy Creek in Llano County. But they do not claim it is very likely.

LLANO COUNTY

This county also was part of the grant the Adelsverein syndicate bought from Fisher and Miller. So the early settlement here, too, was mostly by Germans. The first settlement was at Castell. It was named for one of the officials of the Adelsverein, Count Charles of Castell. Bluffton, on the Colorado, was another early settlement, and it was the largest settlement in the area up until the 1860s.

Settlement at the village that became Llano began about 1855, and this settlement became the county seat when the county was organized from parts of Bexar and Gillespie counties in 1856. The town and the county took their name from the river. The river had been named by the Spanish a good many years earlier. The name means "plain" in Spanish, but some historians think the name may originally have been a corruption of the name of the Lipan Indians, since there are not that many plains around here. The present courthouse in Llano was built in 1892.

Llano County is part of the geological region known as the Llano Uplift, so it is attractive to rockhounds. Prospectors have devoted a good bit of attention to the county over the years, too. The Spanish supposedly dug a little silver and less gold out of the hills here in the early days. Llano County therefore figures in some of the gold legends. Traces of gold have been found in modern times but never in enough volume to justify mining. University of Texas geologists reported in the 1930s that they considered the bed of Sandy Creek in south Llano county about the likeliest spot in the Hill Country for gold. One of the tributaries of Sandy Creek is optimistically named Goldmine Creek. Very little gold has been found in Texas in modern times, and most of what has been found was found by silver miners, mostly in Presidio County. One of the geologists' theories is that veins of gold and silver that may have been in the rocks here once eroded away — years ago.

1   2

1) An imposing monument to the Confederate War dead upstages the courthouse in Llano. The courthouse is one of the old ones, built in 1892. 2) A hotel from the stagecoach days still stands on the courthouse square in Llano. The Southern Hotel was built by J. W. Owens in 1880. It was a stop on the stage line that ran between Mason and Burnet. The hotel is now owned by the Buttery Hardware Company and it has been restored to serve as the company's office.

Gold is the mineral of legends. But the biggest mineral happening in the actual history of Llano County was an iron boom. Northern investors got interested in the iron deposits in the county in the 1880s. Development of the iron mines brought a railroad and telephone service and many new people to Llano County. The boom lasted until 1893. The population of the city of Llano reached 7,300 at the peak. It has been declining since then. The latest census puts it just under 3,000. Mining is not now a factor of any consequence in the economy. Ranching is the principal money maker. The ranchers make some of their money from their livestock and some of it from deer hunters. Llano County usually ranks number one in the state in deer hunting. Or in deer hunters, anyway.

There is a county historical museum at 310 Bessemer Avenue in Llano, and Llano County also has a number of other tourist attractions. The Colorado River forms the eastern boundary of the county, and the western shores of Lake Buchanan, Inks Lake and Lake Lyndon B. Johnson are in Llano County. There are several resorts and fishing camps around Buchanan Lake Village, Golden Beach, Kingsland and Sunrise Beach.

Packsaddle Mountain on State Highway 71 between Llano and Lake Lyndon B. Johnson was the scene of a famous fight

1) *The little lake behind this dam in downtown Llano supplies the city's water. There was a grist mill at the south end of the dam in earlier days.*

2) *A new commercial district developed in north Llano during the boom that followed discovery of iron ore in the late 1800s. The mines closed years ago and some of the boom-days buildings are in ruins.*

2

between settlers and Indians. The real Packsaddle Mountain is in the Big Bend country. This one in Llano County is actually a hill. But it has been called Packsaddle Mountain ever since the settlers and the Indians had it out here in 1873. It was August. A party of about twenty Apaches had been raiding settlements along the Llano, stealing horses and cows. J. R. Moss and seven other settlers trailed the Indians to their camp on top of the mountain and attacked them. Three of the Apaches were killed. The others ran away. The encounter is listed as the last Indian fight in the county's history. Descendants of the victors put a granite marker at the site on top of the mountain in 1938. There is also a state marker on Highway 71, 14 miles southeast of Llano, pointing to the site.

A group of German scholars and intellectuals founded what they called the Communistic Colony of Bettina on the banks of the Llano near the present town of Castell in 1847. Their concept of sharing the work and sharing the wealth failed for the usual reason: More people wanted to share than wanted to work. The colony broke up after less than a year. But some of the members stayed on to become useful citizens in other settlements.

State Highway 16 runs south from Llano to Fredericksburg. There is a state park just off this highway, on Farm Road 965, near the Gillespie County line. The park is new. The attraction is ancient. This is the granite mountain that has been called Enchanted Rock ever since the first settlers learned of the Indian superstitions about it. The granite is not one solid piece. There are cracks and fissures and sometimes

49

1

1) A hill called Packsaddle Mountain got in the history books because some early settlers fought a battle with Indian horse thieves here in 1873. The hill is visible from Highway 71, about 15 miles southeast of Llano. There is a marker on the highway.

2) Packsaddle Mountain today is a launching pad for hang gliders. Glider pilots from Austin, San Antonio and Houston gather here on weekends to ride the air currents on the south side of the hill. The Secret Service put an antenna on top of Packsaddle Mountain while Lyndon Johnson was president so agents could maintain communications between the LBJ Ranch and the President when he was out driving his boat on the lake.

3) Llano County has frontage on three of the Colorado River Lakes and several lakeside resorts with public boat ramps. This is Sunrise Beach on Lake Lyndon B. Johnson.

3

2

1

2

3

1) Enchanted Rock gives hikers a good workout and hiking is the main event at Enchanted Rock State Park.

2) Stone Mountain in Georgia is the biggest rock mountain in the country. Enchanted Rock is the next biggest. It is a dome of granite 325 feet high, spreading over about 70 acres. This was a private resort for many years before it became a state park. There are provisions for picnicking and primitive camping.

3) Marvin Evers' farm is on the north bank of the Llano, opposite the town of Castell. He says the spot where he is standing in this photograph is where the main building of the Communistic Colony of Bettina once stood. Evers remembers there were a few chimney stones here when he was a boy. The founders of Bettina were German intellectuals. Their idea of sharing the work didn't work.

moaning sounds are heard around the place. The Indians invented several legends to explain the moaning and none of their legends made them want to spend much time here. They avoided the area at night. But they apparently were not afraid of it in the daytime. The celebrated Texas Ranger Captain Jack Hays is supposed to have whipped a band of Comanches in a battle on the rock in 1841. The usual explanation for the moaning is that it is the noise the granite blocks make as they contract and grate on each other in the evening after expanding during the heat of the day.

Enchanted Rock was a private tourist resort for many years. The State Department of Parks and Wildlife acquired the rock and the surrounding 1,600 acres in 1979. It is now the Enchanted Rock State Natural Area. There are hiking trails and provisions for picnicking and primitive camping. The admission fee is the usual $2 per vehicle.

1

2

1) There is plenty of stone in Gillespie County and the Germans made good use of it in their early buildings. This one was built in 1881. It was the Gillespie County Courthouse for 58 years. Now it is the Pioneer Memorial Library.
2) The Gillespie County government moved from the stone building in 1939 to this brick building, next door. It is about the most modern building in downtown Fredericksburg.

GILLESPIE COUNTY

Gillespie County is the heart of Texas' German colony, but it was not named for one of the German pioneers. Richard Addison Gillespie came to Texas from Kentucky immediately after Texas won her independence from Mexico. Gillespie joined the Texas Rangers and fought in several skirmishes with Mexicans and Indians during the days of the Republic. He fought with Captain Jack Hays' ranger regiment in the Mexican War, and he was killed in 1846 while leading an attack upon the Bishop's Palace in Monterrey.

The legislature named this county for Captain Gillespie when it was formed from parts of Bexar and Travis counties. The county could as appropriately have been named for John O. Meusebach. He founded the first settlement when he brought 120 German immigrants here from New Braunfels. The establishment of Fredericksburg in 1846 was Meusebach's first major move after he succeeded Prince Carl of Solms-Braunfels as leader of the German colony, and the first step toward the settlement of the more remote lands the Germans had acquired from Henry Fisher and Burchard Miller.

The German founders named Fredericksburg for Prince Frederick of Prussia. The town has been the county seat since the county was organized in 1848. The first courthouse was built in 1855. It is gone, but the courthouse Alfred Giles designed in 1881 is still standing on Main Street. The county government has moved to a newer courthouse, built in 1939. The 1881 courthouse is now a library.

Ranching is the principal occupation in Gillespie County,

The Pioneer Museum on Main Street in Fredericksburg is a small compound including several antique buildings. The main building at 309 West Main was built in the 1850s by Heinrich Kammlah. It was a combination home and general store. Exhibits include furnishings and fixtures from the pioneer days. German tourists often stop here to see the outpost their adventurous countrymen established on the wild frontier. There is a small admission fee.

but there is substantial farming, too. This county produces more peaches than any other county in the state. The orchards around Fredericksburg usually bloom sometime in March. The peaches are ready to eat in August.

An Easter pageant the people of Fredericksburg stage on the Saturday night before Easter grew out of the peace treaty John Meusebach made with the Comanches in March of 1847. The peace conference took place in what is now San Saba County. Bands of Comanches were camped around the little settlement at Fredericksburg waiting for word of the outcome of the pow-wow to be relayed to them by smoke signal. Their campfires lighted up the hills around the town at night. The story is that a German mother, trying to explain all those fires to her children, made up a yarn about Easter bunnies boiling and coloring eggs up in the hills.

The people of Fredericksburg have kept this fairy tale alive ever since, lighting bonfires in the hills around their town on the night before Easter. The pageant evolved from this custom, and it has grown so large that it is held now at the Gillespie County Fairgrounds on the Saturday before Easter.

Another big event in Fredericksburg occurs on the third Saturday in July. They call it "Night in Old Fredericksburg."

1

2

3

1) The Gillespie County peach trees normally bloom sometime in March. Farmers in Gillespie also grow apples, plums, pecans, oats, barley, wheat and corn. But peaches are the chief agricultural product here.

2) The civic and social life of early Fredericksburg revolved around a building the German settlers called the Vereins Kirche. It served as a church and school and community center and it could double as a fort in case of an Indian attack. The original was torn down in 1897, but somebody saved all the plans and this replica was built in the 1930s.

3) The old Nimitz Hotel at 340 East Main has been restored so it again resembles the steamboat that was the original inspiration. The hotel is now a museum. It was built by the late Fleet Admiral Chester Nimitz's grandfather.

It is a festival with German food, German music and German dancing. The churches here still follow a custom they call "Abendglocken." They all ring their bells at six p.m. on Saturdays to remind parishioners of the Sunday services.

Fredericksburg is one of the most picturesque small towns in Texas and conscious of it. One of the first buildings the settlers built here was what they called the Vereins Kirche. It was a combination school and church and community center. The original was torn down in 1897, but a replica was built in 1930, and it is still standing. The replica is just off Main Street, next to the headquarters of the Fredericksburg Chamber of Commerce.

1

2

3

1) The Nimitz Museum has a number of relics of the Pacific campaigns displayed in an open area two blocks from the museum proper. This is a light tank the Japanese used in the fighting on the Pacific islands.
2) Dive bombers like this one were used in the Japanese attack on Pearl Harbor.
3) Admiral Nimitz commanded all U..S. forces in the Pacific. Some Japanese historians regard Nimitz as one of the three greatest admirals of all time. They rank only Lord Nelson and Japan's Heinachiro Togo in Nimitz' class. Japanese craftsmen built this garden for the museum.

One of the original teachers at the original Vereins Kirche in 1847 was Jacob Brodbeck. Some stories say he flew an airplane before the Wright brothers did. There is considerable doubt whether Brodbeck ever flew a plane. But he did hatch an idea for an aircraft powered by coiled springs and a propeller like a ship's screw. This was about 1863. He built a model, and he persuaded some people in Fredericksburg and San Antonio to put up some money to start a factory. But he never raised enough money and the factory never was built. Brodbeck retired to his farm in Gillespie County in 1870 and died there in 1909.

The original settlers of Fredericksburg were allowed a small lot in town and ten acres outside town for a farm. Later settlers only got ten acres outside town, but some of them bought town lots, too. So there is a long tradition here of farmers maintaining some kind of establishment in town. Their houses in town often were very small and occupied only on the weekends because the owners' principal residences were in the country. The farmers would come to town on Saturday to do their shopping and stay over for church and Sunday dinner and a little visiting before returning to the farm Sunday evening. The town houses they built were called

1

2

1) One of the older buildings on Fredericksburg's Main Street is now a gift and souvenir shop featuring articles imported from Germany and Austria. The building was originally the White Elephant Saloon. It was built about 1888. There are antique stores in several of the old buildings along Main Street and shops featuring German sausages and baked goods. TV actor Guich Koock has a German restaurant in an old building that used to be a wagon repair shop.

2) The house at 508 West Main is an example of a Sunday house that was enlarged into a residence. This place is known as the Loeffler-Weber house. The original log section was built in 1846.

3) The Zion Lutheran Church has been standing here at 424 West Main since 1853. Twelve blocks of downtown Fredericksburg are listed in the National Register of Historic Places.

Sunday houses, and many of them are still standing around Fredericksburg. They are identifiable by their small size. They usually have just a living and kitchen area downstairs and a sleeping room upstairs. There is a typical one on the grounds of the Pioneer Museum at 309 West Main. Some of the surviving houses have been enlarged and turned into permanent residences since the automobile changed the way of life that produced the Sunday houses.

The Pioneer Museum at 309 West Main is centered around a combination store and home built by Henry Kammlah. He was one of the original settlers. Exhibits include pioneer furnishings and implements. The museum is open daily during

The late President Lyndon Johnson is buried in the Johnson family cemetery about 15 miles east of Fredericksburg here in Gillespie County. President Johnson died at his home on the LBJ Ranch January 22, 1973, a short distance from the place where he was born 65 years earlier.

the summer months, but only weekends and by appointment the remainder of the year.

A big part of downtown Fredericksburg is listed in the *National Register of Historic Places.* About the most conspicuous building in the historic district is the old Nimitz Hotel. Charles Nimitz came here with the first German settlers. He had been a sailor in German merchant ships for a while before that, and the hotel he built at 340 East Main Street was designed to resemble a ship. Robert E. Lee, Philip Sheridan and Rutherford B. Hayes were among the guests at the Nimitz during its heyday. Charles Nimitz' grandson was born in a house nearby in 1885, and Chester inherited his grandfather's interest in the sea. Chester Nimitz reached the highest rank in the United States Navy and commanded all the U.S. forces in the Pacific in World War II.

The Nimitz Hotel was remodeled and enlarged a number of years ago, and the features that gave it its resemblance to a ship were removed at that time. Those features have been restored now. The hotel looks again something like it did when Charles was running it and Chester was a boy. The hotel is now part of the Admiral Nimitz Center. The Center is a museum preserving Nimitz family mementos and relics of the Pacific war. The Japanese government built a garden on the grounds of the hotel as a tribute to the Admiral after he died. Most of the major war relics are displayed at another site, a couple of blocks from the hotel. The Nimitz Center is open daily from 8:00 to 5:00. The admission fee for visitors over the age of 18 is $1.

Some of the other recorded landmarks here are the White Elephant Saloon at 242 East Main, the Zion Lutheran Church

1

2

3

1) Lyndon Johnson was born August 27, 1908, in a small frame house on the banks of the Pedernales River. President and Mrs. Johnson bought the land years later. It became part of their LBJ Ranch and they rebuilt the little frame house. This part of the ranch is now a National Historic Site. The Park Service conducts bus tours of the ranch every day and there is no charge.

2) Visitors on the bus tour may occasionally see Lady Bird Johnson as their bus passes the main house. She lives in Austin but still spends some time here.

3) One of the buildings on the LBJ Ranch bus tour is the little school house where Lyndon Johnson first attended classes in 1912.

4) There are several historic buildings in the LBJ State Park across the road from the LBJ Ranch. This log cabin was moved here from its original site. The park has picnic tables and a swimming pool. There are no provisions for camping here but camping is allowed in the Lady Bird Johnson Park on State Highway 16, south of Fredericksburg.

4

1) A tiny town with a large reputation is a few miles south of the LBJ Ranch. This is Luckenbach, two houses and a tavern on an unmarked road off Farm Road 1376.

2) One of the best preserved old grist mills in the state is on the bank of Threadgill Creek in northwest Gillespie County. This is Lange's Mill. It is private property, boarded up and posted, but it is right beside a public road. The road is the Lange Mill Road, branching off Farm Road 783, a short distance north of Doss.

at 424 West Main, Admiral Nimitz' birthplace at 247 East Main, the Loeffler-Weber house at 508 West Main, the Montgomery log cabin at 307 West Schubert, and the Knopp house at 309 West Schubert.

Some of the historic houses and buildings are open to the public during the Easter weekend and also on Founders' Day, May 8th.

The late President Lyndon B. Johnson was born in Gillespie County, and he spent the last years of his life here. Johnson's ancestors came to Texas in 1846. His grandfather was in the cattle business in Blanco County, and the future president spent many of his younger years there, at Johnson City. But Lyndon Johnson's mother and father were living in a small house on the Pedernales River in Gillespie County when young Johnson was born. Lyndon and Lady Bird Johnson bought this place years later. They made it part of the LBJ Ranch, and they had the little house where Johnson was born rebuilt as a guest house. The Johnsons gave a large part of the LBJ Ranch, including the little house and the main house and the Johnson family cemetery, to the nation in 1972. This area near Stonewall is now a National Historic Site, administered by the National Park Service. The park service conducts bus tours of the ranch from a base in the Lyndon B. Johnson State Park. The state park occupies most

The founder of Fredericksburg is buried in a little family cemetery near the Christ Lutheran Church at Cherry Spring at the north edge of Gillespie County. The Meusebach cemetery sits back off the road on private property that has several Posted signs on it. But there are several other fine old German stone buildings along the road that leads to this church. It is the Cherry Springs Road, east of U.S. 87, north of Fredericksburg.

of the land between U.S. Highway 290 and Ranch Road 1. It is directly across Ranch Road 1 from the LBJ Ranch and Historic Site. There are some historic buildings in the Lyndon B. Johnson State Park, too, including a farm built by German settler Johann Sauer. There is no admission fee at the Lyndon B. Johnson State Park and no charge, either, for the tours of the ranch. The Johnson property in Blanco County is also a National Historic Site.

President Johnson put Stonewall on the map. Waylon Jennings and Hondo Crouch put Luckenbach on the map, barely. Luckenbach was founded in 1849, but it never grew much, and it was a ghost town by 1970. There was nothing here except two or three empty buildings. Most of us never would have heard of it except that a Hill Country character and story teller named Hondo Crouch bought the town in 1971. Hondo had a knack for dreaming up events that captured the attention of journalists and columnists. He held chili contests and festivals and turned the little settlement into a country and western legend. Luckenbach caught on so that Hondo was able to get national publicity by installing a parking meter. It is rumored that he never saw the place, but Waylon Jennings' recording of "Luckenbach, Texas" helped spread the fame of the little settlement. Hondo died in 1976 and Luckenbach has been less in the news since. But the little general store was still selling beer, and the dance hall was still having occasional dances in 1980. Luckenbach is just off Farm Road 1376 on an unmarked country road. The Highway Department has given up trying to maintain a sign. The signs were stolen as fast as they were put up. But if you are traveling south from U.S. 290 on FM 1376, the turnoff to Luckenbach is to the right. It is not one of those places you can't miss.

1) *Kerrville was originally called Kerrsville. The city and Kerr County both were named for surveyor James Kerr. The present courthouse in Kerrville was built in 1926 and added to in 1977.*

2) *Cypress trees still grow in the Guadalupe near Hunt. These trees attracted the first settlers here. They wanted the wood for shingles. This drive, on Farm Road 1340, is as pretty as any in Texas.*

2

KERR COUNTY

Kerr County is the part of Texas most favored by many Texans from other parts of the state. Many successful Texans have ranches and summer homes here. There are camps for young people, resorts and artists' colonies. Cowboy cartoonist Ace Reid and western singer Floyd Tillman live here. The summer climate is pleasant. The scenery is fine.

The Guadalupe River rises in this county. The river gives the county much of its beauty and character, and the cypress trees along the Guadalupe brought the first white settlers here. The first settler probably was Joshua Brown. He brought a small party here from the settlement at Gonzales in 1848. They came to make shingles from the cypress trees. Their little settlement was known as Brownsborough at first. The name was changed to Kerrsville when Kerr County was organized in 1856. Kerrsville gradually came to be called Kerrville. The town and the county both were named for James Kerr. He probably never set foot on any part of what is now Kerr County. But James Kerr was surveyor for the Green C. DeWitt Colony, one of the founders of Gonzales and a friend of Joshua Brown's.

Kerrville was the original county seat. The government moved to Comfort in 1860, but it came back to Kerrville because Comfort was included in Kendall County when Kendall County was organized in 1862. Kerrville has been the

1) *Charles Schreiner made the first big money in Kerr County. He came here from France in the early 1850s. He borrowed the money to start a general store after the Civil War. It succeeded and Schreiner went into banking and buying and selling wool.*

2) *Schreiner built an elaborate home next door to his store and he had a tunnel between the store and the house. The Schreiner mansion is listed in the* National Register of Historic Places *and it is now being restored.*

3) *The Schreiner family has a collection of antiques and old buildings at the Y.O. Ranch. The place is stocked with native and exotic game. Guests can stay here at the lodge and hunt, for a price. The Y.O. Ranch is west of Mountain Home, off State Highway 41.*

county seat ever since. The present courthouse was built in 1926 and the addition in 1977.

The early settlers here had their share of troubles with the Indians. Comanches, Apaches and Kiowas roamed the territory. They killed a number of the pioneers. Clara Watkins' *Kerr County, Texas, 1856-1976* says the last Indian raid, on the James Dowdy farm on the Guadalupe in 1878, claimed the lives of four of the Dowdy children.

Ranching and entertaining visitors and tourists are the principal occupations in Kerr County. Sheep and goats were introduced here about as early as anywhere in Texas, so Kerrville was one of the first wool and mohair centers. And Charles Schreiner was one of the first wool brokers.

Schreiner was born in France. He came to Texas in 1852. He served three years in the Texas rangers and then started a ranch in Kerr County. Schreiner opened a general store in

The peace and beauty of the Guadalupe Valley attracts artists and artisans of all kinds. Many accomplished painters and print makers, sculptors and designers of wall hangings, custom jewelers and potters have homes and studios along the river between Hunt and Center Point. Some of the homes and studios are open to the public during the annual Hill Country Fine Arts Trail around the first of October each year. Some of the artists' work is usually on display at the Hill Country Arts Foundation at Ingram. The Arts Foundation also conducts art classes and an outdoor summer theater program here.

Kerrville after the Civil War. He branched out into banking and the wool business and became the richest man in the area before he died in 1927. The home Charles Schreiner built in 1879 still stands at 216 Earl Garrett Street in Kerrville, and the Schreiner Institute he founded in 1919 is still operating as Schreiner College. Schreiner's heirs and descendants are still active in the management of the Schreiner enterprises including the Y. O. Ranch in northwest Kerr County. The Y. O. is a working ranch and a guest ranch, too. It is stocked with several species of exotic animals. Visitors can arrange to hunt some of these as well as the native white tailed deer. The entrance to the Y. O. Ranch is off State Highway 41, about 14 miles west of Mountain Home.

The Hill Country Arts Foundation was established in 1958 beside the Guadalupe in Ingram. The foundation conducts art classes and summer theater programs. There is a restaurant and gallery. Several artists live and work in the area between Ingram and Comfort, and some of their studios are open to the public in the early fall during the Hill Country Fine Arts Trail program. You can get dates and details from the Chamber of Commerce, Box 790, Kerrville 78028.

1

1) *The upper Guadalupe is lined with private retreats, summer homes, childrens' camps and commercial resorts of various degrees. The River Inn at Hunt sits beside a dam that forms a small lake for the guests to swim in.*
2) *The Kerrville State Park south of Kerrville has provisions for swimming and fishing and camping. There are 23 screened shelters for rent in the park. One section of the park is on the Guadalupe River and the other section is on a hill on the opposite side of State Highway 173.*

2

Kerr County has a great variety of resorts ranging from the Inn of the Hills in Kerrville and the River Inn at Hunt to the Kerrville State Park on State Highway 173, three miles south of Kerrville.

The park is one of the Class I state parks with the usual admission fee of $2 per vehicle if you do not have the annual permit or the Senior Citizens' Passport. The park is on the Guadalupe. There are provisions for swimming, fishing and picnicking. There are 65 campsites and 23 screened shelters for rent. The address for reservations or more information is 2385 Bandera Highway, Kerrville 78028.

The Classic Car Showcase and Wax Museum at Interstate 10 and Farm Road 783, northwest of Kerrville, is a private museum featuring some rare old cars and wax likenesses of old film stars. It is closed Mondays. There is an admission fee.

The U.S. Army established a number of forts along the frontier to protect settlers and travelers after Texas joined the Union, and Kerr County got one of those outposts. It was called Camp Verde, and it was on Verde Creek, south of Kerrville. Camp Verde had the distinction of being the only

1

2

1) The Classic Car Showcase is a museum on the western edge of Kerrville. The exhibits here are wax likenesses of some of the old-time screen stars and a collection of old automobiles in showroom condition. This Isotta-Fraschini is reputed to be exactly like one the late Rudolph Valentino used to drive.
2) The Mooney Aircraft Corporation builds sleek business airplanes in a plant at the Kerrville Municipal Airport, off State Highway 27. The Mooney plant offers tours for visitors Mondays through Thursdays at 2 p.m.

camel base on the frontier. Secretary of War Jefferson Davis engineered the purchase of a herd of camels in 1855. The idea was to find out whether it would be practical to use camels as pack animals in the west instead of horses and mules. The camels were brought to Camp Verde, and there were several caravans from here to various posts farther out on the frontier. The Civil War interrupted the experiment. Texas Confederates took over Camp Verde. They used some of the camels to haul cotton to Brownsville. Some reports say the camels were all scattered when the U.S. Army returned to Camp Verde after the war. Other reports say there were more camels here at the end of the war than there had been at the start. But the camel experiment was not resumed. One Southern theory is that the U.S. let the experiment die because the author of it became the president of the Confederate States. The Jefferson Davis connection may have been a factor, but it was also clear by the end of the Civil War that railroads were going to replace pack animals. Reports on the camels' performance as pack animals were generally very good.

The army abandoned Camp Verde in 1869. The property has been in private hands for many years now. One of the old buildings has been rebuilt to serve as a residence. Nothing is left of the camel barns. And there is not much left of the town of Camp Verde except the Camp Verde General Store. Lewis Lackey and his son, Lamar, are still turning out cypress lumber at the old fashioned Triple L Sawmill off U.S. 173 near here.

1) *The U.S. Army bought a herd of camels in the 1850s to find out if they would be better pack animals than horses on the western frontier. The camels were based at Camp Verde in southern Kerr County.*

2) *The experiment was not unsuccessful but it was interrupted by the Civil War. Then the railroads came and nobody needed camels. The land where Camp Verde was is now a private ranch. The gate and the state marker are about the only evidence that the camp was here. They are on an unmarked county road just west of Highway 173.*

3) *The old Camp Verde General Store is still doing business here, on the opposite side of Highway 173. There is a pleasant little roadside park and picnic spot on the creekbank in front of the store.*

BLANCO COUNTY

Blanco County is another area that owes much of its fame to the late President Johnson. But the president's ancestors had put the Johnson name on the map here long before the president was born. Sam Ealy Johnson Sr., and his brother, Tom, had a cattle empire here during the days before the first fences. They rounded up longhorns on the open range and drove them up the Chisholm Trail to market in the 1860s. The Johnson brothers made their headquarters in a log cabin near the present site of Johnson City before there was a city. Sam Ealy Johnson Sr. was Lyndon Johnson's grandfather and one of his heroes.

Johnson City was named for the Johnsons when it was founded in 1878. Johnson City became the county seat of Blanco County in 1891. The county was organized in 1858 from parts of Burnet, Comal, Gillespie and Hays counties. The name was taken from the Blanco River, and the river was named by one of the early Spanish explorers in the 1700s. Blanco is Spanish for white. The town of Blanco was the

1) Johnson City was named for the ancestors of the late President Lyndon Johnson. President Johnson was born in Gillespie County, but he spent most of his boyhood years here in Johnson City. The Johnson home is now a National Historic Site managed by the National Park Service.
2) The park service provides wagons to carry visitors from the house in Johnson City to the little settlement where the late president's grandfather lived in the 1860s.
3) Sam Ealy Johnson's log house was built by another early settler in 1856.

county seat until 1891. The building that was the courthouse is still standing in the center of Blanco. It has been used for a variety of purposes since the government left. The second floor was even a skating rink for a while. The first judge to hold court in Blanco was E. J. Davis. He later became the first Republican governor of Texas during the "Reconstruction."

The Blanco State Park on the Blanco River just off U.S.

1   2

1) Johnson City has been the county seat of Blanco County since the residents of the county voted to move the county government here in 1891. The present courthouse was designed by Henry Phelps and built in 1916. The exterior looks original except for the composition roof.
2) The original county seat for Blanco County was the town of Blanco. The stone courthouse county officials built in Blanco in 1885 is still standing.

281 at the southern edge of the town of Blanco has provisions for camping, picnicking, swimming and fishing. This is one of the state's Class I parks, with the usual admission fee and additional charges for campsites. The Blanco park has half a dozen screened shelters and more than thirty campsites. The address for reservations or additional information is Box 493, Blanco 78606.

One building in Blanco is listed in the *National Register of Historic Places*. It is the Adrian Edwards Conn house on U.S. 281 at the town square. This building is typical of those built by the pioneer German settlers in these hills. It is limestone with outside walls more than a foot thick.

Lyndon Johnson's mother and father moved from their house on the Pedernales to a frame house in Johnson City when the future president was five years old. Lyndon Johnson grew up in this house, and he made his first political speech from the front porch here the first time he ran for office in 1937. The house is between 9th and 10th streets in Johnson City, one block off U.S. 281. It has been restored. The National Park Service has charge of this home and the site of the original Johnson settlement. The original log home of the first Johnsons has been restored, too, and there are several other historic buildings in the original settlement just west of the house on 9th Street. The house and the settlement both are open to visitors daily. There is no fee.

Visitors can easily walk the short distance between the house and the original Johnson settlement, but they may also

1) Rock fences once were common in this part of Texas. The farmers had
*rocks before they had barbed wire. A few rock fences still stand in Blanco
County, but they are mostly falling down.*
2) Blanco has one old house listed in the National Register of Historic Places.
*This is the Adrian Conn house at 3rd and Main on the courthouse square. It
is private property.*

ride if they wish in the replicas of early Texas freight wagons
the Park Service operates. The Johnsons gave the government
the president's boyhood home and the money to buy the other
property here. Lyndon Johnson was proud of his pioneer
ancestors. He brought many rich and famous people here and
told them how his grandmother used to hide under the log
cabin when the Indians were on the warpath. He wanted these
sites preserved to remind future generations of our ancestors'
early struggles.

Ranching is still the main business here, but prospectors
have worked parts of Blanco County over pretty thoroughly.
It has been rumored since frontier days that there once was a
gold mine in this area. It is recorded that frontiersman Jim
Bowie spent some time looking for gold along the San Saba
River before he was killed at the Alamo. It is not recorded
that he ever found a gold mine. But some of his associates
believed he did have some access to gold. They claimed he
often had some on him. Somebody said that somebody said
that Bowie told somebody he had a secret mine near the headwaters of Cow Creek. About a dozen creeks in Texas have
this name, but somebody concluded that the Cow Creek in
what is now Blanco County was the one where the Bowie
mine was. This creek is a tributary of the Pedernales River.
Plenty of people have looked, but nobody's found any gold.

A couple from Austin has turned an old stagecoach inn in
Round Mountain into a home. Colonel and Mrs. Richard
Hernlund are restoring the old building that was known as the
Martin Hotel when it was new in 1874.

1

2

1) *The Blanco State Park on the southern edge of the town of Blanco has frontage on both sides of the Blanco River. The park is on U.S. 281.*
2) *The former Circle Bar Ranch northeast of Johnson City is now a state park. The principal attraction in the Pedernales Falls State Park is the Pedernales River. The park entrance is on Ranch Road 3232 off U.S. 290, east of Johnson City. These are Class I parks with the usual entrance fees.*
3) *Lawrence O'Brian took the oath of office as Postmaster General here at the Hye Post Office in 1965. It was President Johnson's idea.*
4) *Stagecoaches on the run between Johnson City and Marble Falls used to make regular stops at a place called the Birdtown Inn in what is now called Round Mountain. The stone building is now a private residence.*

3

4

There is another state park in Blanco County, on the Pedernales River, east of Johnson City. The entrance to the Pedernales Falls State Park is off Ranch Road 2766. This is a Class I park with the usual fees. The location is outstanding. There are provisions for swimming, fishing and picnicking and about 90 campsites for rent. The address for reservations and information is Route 1, Box 31A, Johnson City 78636.

The Pedernales Falls State Park includes a very good hiking trail about seven miles long.

The San Marcos River begins in a cluster of springs in the city of San Marcos. The Aquarena Springs Park envelopes the pool created by these springs. This is the view of the headwaters of the San Marcos from the Aquarena Springs sky ride.

HAYS COUNTY

Signs on all the major highways in this part of the state invite travelers to visit Aquarena Springs in San Marcos. Aquarena Springs is a very commercial resort. But there is a lot of history in San Marcos and Hays County, too. Many of the early explorers and settlers came through here, and there was an Indian campground long before that. The attraction was the same then as now. There is an abundance of good water. The springs that feed the San Marcos River produce millions of gallons of clear, cool water every day.

The early Spanish explorers gave the San Marcos River its name. This may have been another one of those cases where the name originally was intended for another stream. But this stream has been known as the San Marcos at least since 1709. The spring was a regular stop by that time on the Old San Antonio Road, also known as the Camino Real. The road was established in 1691 to link the provincial capital of Monclova with the Spanish missions on the Louisiana border. The Spanish missions San Francisco Xavier de los Dolores, Nuestra Señora de la Candelaria and San Ildefonso were located here temporarily (1755 to 1757). And a few Spanish families came here from Mexico in 1808 to establish a settlement they called San Marcos de Neve. Indian raids compelled those colonists to give up and return to Mexico in 1812. The

1

1) The annual Texas Water Safari canoe race begins at the Aquarena Springs Hotel. Contestants paddle from here all the way to the coast. People are not permitted to paddle their canoes in the San Marcos River at Aquarena Springs except on very special occasions like this. But there is a public park just downstream from Aquarena Springs where you can rent canoes and floats and paddle all you like.

2) The first people here settled by the water. One of the very first was Eli Merriman. He built this house in 1846. It is now part of Aquarena Springs Park.

2

first Anglo settlers started coming in about 1847, and the town that became San Marcos was founded by William Lindsey, Edward Burleson and Eli T. Merriman. Burleson was one of the earliest settlers here. He had come to Texas in 1830. He commanded the first regiment of Texas Volunteers at San Jacinto. He served in the Congress of the Republic, and he was vice president of Texas during Sam Houston's second term as president.

General Burleson was serving in the State Senate when he moved his family to this area in 1848. He introduced the legislation that created Hays County that year. San Marcos has been the county seat from the beginning. The present courthouse was built in 1909. The county was named for the noted Texas ranger and Indian fighter Captain John Coffee "Jack" Hays. Hays was a nephew of U.S. President Andrew Jackson. He came to Texas in 1837. He fought with the Rangers against the Indians on the frontier and against the Mexicans during the Mexican War. He moved to California the year after this county was named for him, and he later founded the city of Oakland.

1) The Aquarena Springs Park is open the year around and the Wonder Cave in south San Marcos is also open every day of the year. The Wonder Cave is on Bishop Street. You get there by taking Exit 202 from Interstate 35 and following the signs. There are tours of the cave every 15 minutes. The admission fee covers the other attractions in Wonder World Park.
2) The legislature authorized a teachers' school for San Marcos in 1899. The original name was Southwest Texas Normal School. It is now Southwest Texas State University. One of the teachers trained here was Lyndon Johnson.

Hays never lived here, but General Burleson did. He built a double log cabin at the head of the San Marcos. He built the first dam across the river and he operated a grist mill and sawmill here for a time. The Burleson log cabin rotted away and collapsed a number of years ago. It was rebuilt in the 1960s with some of the original chimney stones and logs from some other old buildings in the area. The Aquarena Springs Park now occupies the land that was the Burleson property, and the rebuilt Burleson cabin is one of the features in the park. The park also includes Eli Merriman's old log home.

A. B. Rogers started developing the resort at Aquarena Springs in the 1920s. The resort had some ups and downs, and it was closed a couple of times before Rogers hit upon the idea of putting in boats with glass bottoms so visitors could gaze down at the fish and aquatic plants. That idea put Aquarena Springs in the big league. Other attractions have been added, but the boats with the windows in the bottom are still very popular. There are admission fees for each of the attractions. Visitors may also buy combination tickets that will admit them to all the attractions. There is a small hotel on the

1) *Southwest Texas State has grown so much that it has taken over the original campus of the San Marcos Baptist Academy. The Academy is developing a new campus farther out on the road to Wimberly. San Marcos Academy was founded in 1906 to teach boys and girls from the first grade through high school. This building on the original campus was built in 1907.*

2) *San Marcos has been the county seat since Hays County was established in 1848. The present courthouse is the fourth one the county has had. It was built in 1909 and restored in 1972.*

3) *The legislature named this county for Captain Jack Hays. He was one of the most famous Texas Rangers.*

3

grounds. The San Marcos River is very popular with divers because the water is so clear. But divers are not allowed in the Aquarena Springs Park.

One of the major events in canoeing begins here at Aquarena Springs every June. This is the starting point of the Texas Water Safari. This canoe race draws entrants from all over the country. They paddle down the San Marcos to the Guadalupe and down the Guadalupe to the Gulf at Seadrift.

The Wonder Cave on Bishop Street in San Marcos is open every day, and there are tours every 15 minutes. The cave is listed as having been discovered in 1893, but it probably was known to the Indians and the Spaniards before that.

The late President Lyndon B. Johnson got his college education here in San Marcos. He started classes at the Southwest Texas State Teachers' College in 1927, and he was graduated in 1930 from the school that is known now as Southwest Texas State University. The boarding house where Johnson lived while he was a student still stands at 400 Lyndon Baines Johnson Drive. The school has grown

One of the recorded landmarks in San Marcos is the house Charles Cock built in 1867. The little stone and frame house is listed in the National Register of Historic Places. *The area was a farm when Cock built the house, but it has turned urban and the farmhouse now has a street address. It is 402 East Hopkins.*

substantially since Johnson's days, and the campus now includes the original site of the San Marcos Baptist Academy. The Academy is moving to a new location.

The original buildings of both schools are recorded Texas landmarks, and a number of other buildings in San Marcos and Hays County have been awarded historical markers. The Cock house at 402 East Hopkins in San Marcos is listed in the *National Register of Historic Places*. So is the First United Methodist Church at 129 West Hutchinson in San Marcos. The First Baptist Church at 330 West Hutchinson and the First Presbyterian Church at Hutchinson and Mary have Texas historical markers as does the Ragsdale house at 621 West San Antonio.

Antique collectors and flea market buffs converge on Wimberly on the first Saturday of each month between May and October. First Saturday is Market Day in Wimberly. Work produced by the local artists and craftsmen is offered for sale along with antiques and barnyard relics. Wimberly is a popular summer resort situated about as picturesquely as any town in the Hill Country.

The community was settled in 1848. The first settler was a miller named William Winters. The mill Winters built on the Blanco was bought by Pleasant Wimberly in 1874, and the settlement took his name when the post office was established in 1880. The mill was altered several times before it was finally closed in 1934. There is only a marker at the site, near the Wimberly Bank.

Pioneer Town, outside Wimberly, has a collection of authentic old buildings and replicas arranged to resemble an old time western village. Pioneer Town is open every day. There is an admission fee.

If you are going to Austin from here, you might try Farm Road 3247 east to Farm Road 150 and go north on 150 to

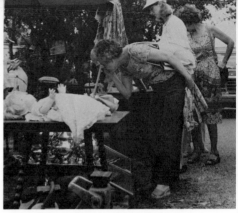

1) The 7A Ranch Resort on the Blanco River one mile outside of Wimberly includes a frontier village called Pioneer Town. The village is made up of replicas of pioneer saloons and stores and a couple of authentic old log cabins. This is a guest ranch with rooms and cabins for rent.
2) A big flea market draws thousands of people to Wimberly on the first Saturday of each month from May through October.
3) Thomas Johnson founded a school on Bear Creek in 1852. Johnson Institute closed in 1872. The building is now the headquarters of the Friday Mountain Boys' Camp.

Driftwood and turn east there onto Farm Road 1826 until it joins U.S. 290 just west of Austin. This is a pleasant drive, and it will take you by Friday Mountain Ranch. The old rock building at Friday Mountain Ranch was built in 1852 to house a school known as Johnson Institute. Historian Walter Prescott Webb bought the place and restored it in 1942, and it became the headquarters of the Friday Mountain Boys' Camp. Friday Mountain is on FM 1826 at Bear Creek.

One of the popular swimming holes in the Hill Country is Blue Hole, a half mile outside Wimberly. This resort is on Cypress Creek off the old Kyle Road. It is privately owned. There is an admission fee for swimmers and additional charges for the campsites and trailer sites.

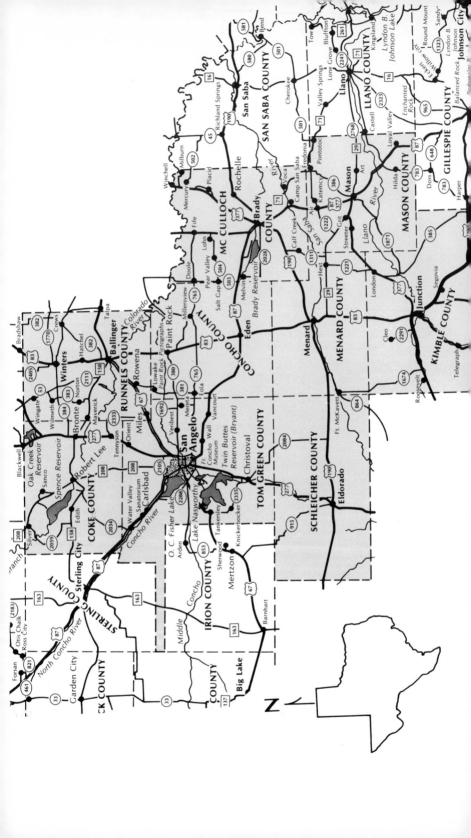

San Angelo area

Tom Green, Coke, Runnels, Concho,
McCulloch, Menard, Mason, Kimble,
Schleicher and Irion counties.

This is the heart of the Texas sheep and goat country. Spanish explorers came to this part of Texas as early as the 1500s, and they may have mined some gold here, but the area was a long time being settled. Indians continued to be a problem until the late 1870s.

The Butterfield-Overland Stage Line came through here. Some of the forts the U.S. Army built to protect the frontier in the 1850s were here. Robert E. Lee was stationed here.

Jim Bowie killed Indians here. The late Governor Coke Stevenson was born here. So was Clyde Barrow's friend, Bonnie Parker.

Tom Green County is named for Confederate General Tom Green. He never lived in this area but he fought in all of Texas' wars until he was killed in a Civil War battle in 1864, ten years before this county was established.

TOM GREEN COUNTY

The area that is now Tom Green County was an important base during the final stage of the Indian war on the Texas frontier. It was beyond the frontier until after the Civil War.

The Butterfield Stage Line began running through here in 1858. The coaches from St. Louis came south from Fort Chadbourne in what is now Coke County and turned westward here to follow the valley of the Middle Concho River toward the Pecos and California. There were a few stage stands, but no settlements. Stage service was suspended when the Civil War began. U.S. troops left the frontier forts. The Indians had this country to themselves. The first permanent white settler didn't come here until 1864, and he was taking a big chance.

Texas frontier guards took over responsibility for the security of the frontier during the Civil War. Some of these guards and some Confederate troops lost a major skirmish with the Indians here in January of 1865. The guards found the remains of a large, fresh Indian campsite, and they jumped to the conclusion that they had found the trail of a Comanche war party. They followed the trail. They found a band of Indians and pounced on them. The Indians were Kickapoos. There were more than a thousand of them, and they were making a move from the Oklahoma Indian Territory to Mexico. They were not looking for trouble, but they were well armed, and they fought back when the party of 370 Texans attacked them. The Texans gave up the attack after losing 36 men. The Kickapoos buried eleven men and went on to Mexico.

It was called the Battle of Dove Creek. It was fought about sixteen miles south of the present city of San Angelo. It did not encourage settlers, and there was no serious settlement here until the U.S. Army returned to the frontier forts at the end of the Civil War. The Army decided the water supply at

1

1) David Dary says in his "Buffalo Book" that the systematic slaughter of the buffalo for their hides began in this part of Texas about 1874 and lasted until about 1878. The hides were worth about 3 dollars apiece at the time. The elimination of the buffalo herds deprived the plains Indians of their food supply and forced them onto reservations.

2) This lady gave her name to the settlement that became San Angelo. Her name was Angela and when her sister's husband started his trading post outside Fort Concho, he called it Santa Angela. But people found it easier to say San Angelo.

2

Fort Chadbourne was not reliable, so Fort Chadbourne was closed. The troops were moved from there to a new fort here on the Concho River in 1867. Fort Concho was built at the junction of the Concho and the North Concho. The fort attracted settlers. B. J. Dewitt established a trading post across the river from the fort. He named it Santa Angela in honor of his wife's sister, and by the time the settlement became a town, it was being called San Angelo.

This whole area was still part of the original Bexar District until 1874 when the legislature created a new county and named it Tom Green. The new county originally covered a huge area that has since been divided into 13 counties. The county was named for a veteran of the Battle of San Jacinto. Thomas Green was a private in the Texas revolutionary army. He was a captain in the war with Mexico, and he became a brigadier general in the Confederate Army before he was killed in 1864. Green commanded part of the force that recaptured Galveston from the Union troops in 1863.

1) San Angelo has not always been the county seat for Tom Green County. The county government was established originally at a settlement called Ben Ficklin. It moved to San Angelo after a flood on the South Concho washed Ben Ficklin away. The present courthouse in San Angelo was built in 1927 when Americans were feeling especially prosperous.

2) Two brothers named Ruffini designed many of the courthouses and jails and public buildings in Texas in the late 1800s. F. E. Ruffini lived and worked in Austin. His brother Oscar lived and worked here in San Angelo. Oscar Ruffini designed more than 3 dozen of San Angelo's buildings. This one on South Chadbourne Street and several of the other Ruffini buildings were being restored during the 1970s.

2

The original county seat here was the settlement of Ben Ficklin on the South Concho about four miles from the settlement that became San Angelo. Ben Ficklin was a stage line operator and mail contractor. He obtained a government contract after the Civil War ended to haul the mail between Fort Smith, Arkansas, and El Paso. Ficklin established his headquarters and shops on the South Concho. He had a number of people working for him, and when it came time to vote for a county seat, those people voted for their boss' town. The county government remained at Ben Ficklin until 1882 when a flood destroyed the settlement and killed 65 people. The government moved then to San Angelo. The Santa Fe

1

1) Construction of Fort Concho began in 1867. There were thirty stone buildings here by the time the Army abandoned the fort in 1889.

2) Colonel Ranald Mackenzie was in command of Fort Concho in 1871 when he received the orders making him responsible for the final solution of the Indian problem on the frontier. His troops killed Indians for 5 years. The survivors moved to the reservations in Oklahoma and white settlers moved in to claim the land.

3) The city of San Angelo owns Fort Concho now. Twenty-two of the buildings are still standing. The museum on the grounds has a number of displays of military gear and relics and photographs from the frontier days. The Fort Concho Museum is open Tuesdays through Saturdays and on Sunday afternoons.

2   3

1) The E. H. Danner Museum of Telephony has a collection of antique communications equipment on display. The museum is in the new General Telephone Company building in San Angelo. It is open during regular office hours, Mondays through Fridays, and there is no admission charge. San Angelo is General Telephone's hometown.

2) A marker at the site of the first farm in what is now Tom Green County recalls that the principal customers for farm products in the 1860s in this area were the frontier forts. What is left of the Bismarck Farm is about 5 miles southwest of San Angelo, on Fish Hatchery Road.

railroad came through San Angelo in 1888, and the city has been growing ever since. The present courthouse in San Angelo was built in 1927.

San Angelo calls itself the "Sheep and Wool Capital." Sheep, goat and cattle ranches are major factors in the economy here. But there is some oil and gas, too, and some manufacturing. Irrigated farms here were growing food and feed for the frontier forts by the middle 1870s. But the principal business in Tom Green County in the 1870s was hunting buffalo. N. A. Taylor wrote in his account of his travels in Texas, *2,000 Miles in Texas on Horseback,* that he saw a herd of buffalo here in 1877 so big it extended to the horizon. A very few years later the buffalo were all gone. White hunters slaughtered them wholesale for their hides. This slaughter was one of the factors contributing to bad feelings between the Indians and the whites. The Indians relied upon the buffalo for food.

The U.S. government was following a policy of paternalism toward the Indians by the 1870s. Most of the Indians from the eastern states had been pushed onto reservations in Oklahoma, and the policy was to coerce the Texas Indians to move to the reservations, too. But Indians were still killing settlers in Texas, and some of the killers were Indians ostensibly living on the reservations. Settlers in west Texas complained that the Indians were being coddled. They wanted a firmer policy, and they got it. The U.S. Army's top general

The Goodyear Tire and Rubber Company used to test its tires on Texas highways. The company built a proving ground outside San Angelo in 1958 and this is now the principal test area for Goodyear tires. The proving ground is not open to visitors, but group tours can be arranged through Goodyear offices.

came to Texas in 1871 to inspect the frontier. General William T. Sherman traveled from San Antonio to Fort Sill, Oklahoma. He saw several ranches and settlements that had been abandoned because of Indian raids. And Sherman and his party were near Fort Griffin on May 18th, when a party of Kiowas and Comanches attacked a wagon train commanded by Captain Henry Warren in the same area. The raiders killed seven teamsters. Sherman happened to be at Fort Sill a short time later when the Kiowa chief Satanta returned to the reservation there boasting that he had led the attack on the Warren wagon train. The general's Indian policy was different from then on. He ordered Colonel Ranald Mackenzie to make war on the Indians. Fort Concho was one of the bases Mackenzie used in that war.

Fort Concho is one of the best preserved of the old Texas frontier forts. Part of it is now a museum open to visitors every day.

Two of the badmen of the 1890s came from here. Tom and Sam Ketchum did most of their mischief in Arizona and New Mexico, but they were born and raised at Knickerbocker in southwest Tom Green County. The Ketchum Boys' specialty was holding up trains, and it got them both killed. Sam was fatally wounded in a shootout with a posse after he held up a passenger train near Folsom, Arizona in 1899. Tom was wounded and captured after he robbed a train in the same area a few months later. Tom was hanged for his crimes in 1901.

1

2

3

1) The Goodfellow Air Force Base in San Angelo has been training airmen since 1941. The base was named for Lieutenant James Goodfellow Jr. He was one of the American flyers killed in France in World War I.

2) Mitsubishi of Japan assembles business airplanes in a plant at Mathis Field. There is no tour schedule, but visitors are tolerated.

3) There are provisions for swimming, fishing, picnicking and camping at Lake Nasworthy, off U.S. 67 about 6 miles southwest of San Angelo. This is one of the three lakes supplying water for San Angelo.

4) The little town of Christoval on U.S. 277 south of San Angelo is the home of one of Daniel Boone's descendants. Pecos Pate Boone says Daniel was his great grandfather. Pecos Pate used to have his own traveling wild west show. Now he makes custom knives and spurs and sells antiques and tells stories. Christoval is a former resort. There were mineral baths here.

4

Some of the old frontier forts in West Texas are parks and most of them are accessible. But old Fort Chadbourne is not. This is private property and tourists are not welcome. Fort Chadbourne was established in 1852 and abandoned in 1867. The ruins are on a ranch in northeast Coke County, off U.S. 277.

COKE COUNTY

The defense of this section of the Texas frontier pivoted on a base in what is now Coke County before Fort Concho was built in what is now Tom Green County.

The U.S. Army established Fort Chadbourne on Oak Creek in 1852 to protect the frontier and the road to California. Most of the army's frontier posts were named for servicemen killed in the war with Mexico. This one was named for Lieutenant Theodore Chadbourne. He was killed at Resaca de la Palma in 1846. Fort Chadbourne became a way station on the Butterfield Overland Mail line when it was established in 1858. Confederate forces occupied Chadbourne during the Civil War. Federal troops returned after the war, but they moved from here to Fort Concho in 1867 and Fort Chadbourne fell into ruins.

Cattlemen began settling here in the 1860s. The county was formed in 1889 from part of Tom Green County. It was named for Governor Richard Coke. Governor Coke was the Democrat elected in 1873 to succeed Republican E. J. Davis. Unionists and carpetbaggers had backed Davis, and he disputed the legality of the election Coke won. He refused to give up the governor's office until President U.S. Grant made it clear he was not going to use federal troops to keep Davis in office. The election of Coke marked the end of carpetbag rule in Texas, so he was something of a hero to Southern sympathizers. And the county seat of Coke County is named for the chief Southern hero.

Two veterans of the Confederate Army founded the town in 1889 and named it for their commander, Robert E. Lee.

1

2

3

1) *A little settlement grew up near Fort Chadbourne when it was an active fort. The rail line that came through here was called the Historic Route because it followed the old Butterfield Stage route, more or less. The ruin of a depot on the old Historic Route stands on an unmarked dirt road north of Bronte.*
2) *The principal town in Coke County when the county was established in 1889 was a settlement called Hayrick. The town was named for a hill that resembles a hayrick. Residents of the town of Robert Lee promoted an election in 1891 and got the county seat moved to Robert Lee. Hayrick Mountain is still here, but nothing is left of the town of Hayrick except the cemetery, on a county road, about 5 miles east of Robert Lee.*
3) *Two Confederate veterans founded the town of Robert Lee and they named it for the Confederate general, shown here in the uniform of a Lieutenant Colonel of the U.S. Army, before the war.*

The original county seat here was a small town named Hayrick. But there was an election in 1891, and the people voted to move the government to Robert Lee. The decision turned Hayrick into a ghost town, but it didn't exactly turn Robert Lee into a boomtown. The population hovers around 1,000. The present courthouse was built in 1956.

The ruins of old Fort Chadbourne are in the northeastern corner of the county, just off U.S. 277, about 12 miles north of Bronte. Only a few rock walls remain at the site. Nothing much is left, either, of the town of Fort Chadbourne that grew up outside the military post in the early days. The town of Bronte was not established until 1887, long after Fort Chadbourne was abandoned. It owes its survival mainly to being on the railroad. Bronte was named for the English novelist Charlotte Bronte, author of *Jane Eyre*. Coke County also has a little town named Tennyson for the English poet.

Coke County is the eastern edge of the Permian Basin. The

1

2

1) *The Coke County government has been based in Robert Lee since 1891. It has been in this courthouse since 1956.*

2) *A marker on the courthouse grounds at Robert Lee reminds us that the cow country around here did not make the transition from the open range days to the era of fences and firm property lines without some grief. Many fences were destroyed and some people were killed before the old time cowmen recognized the right of property owners to fence their property.*

3) *Robert Lee was founded by Confederate veterans and the name apparently attracted other Confederate veterans here. Thirty-four Confederate veterans and one Union veteran are buried in the Robert Lee Cemetery.*

3

first oil was found here in 1942. There is substantial oil and gas production now, but ranching is still an important factor in the economy of Coke County.

1

2

1) Runnels County had an experience similar to that of several other Texas counties. The builders of the first railroad didn't happen to lay their tracks through the town that was serving as the county seat. The county seat when the Gulf, Colorado and Santa Fe came through the county was Runnels. The railroad established a new town, 5 miles to the south, and named it Ballinger. 2) The Runnels County government moved from Runnels to Ballinger in 1887. The courthouse in Ballinger was built two years later.

RUNNELS COUNTY

Runnels County was created from parts of Bexar and Travis counties in 1858 and organized in 1880. There was a Spanish mission here much earlier. The Mission San Clemente was established here in 1684. The missionaries built only a rough log building before the Apaches drove them off. Nothing remains of San Clemente, and there is some doubt about the exact site, but there is an historical marker at the approximate site, east of U.S. 83, about 20 miles southeast of Ballinger. This was the first Spanish mission east of the Pecos.

The first Anglo settlers came here in the early 1860s, and the first settlement was Picketville near the present town of Ballinger. The first settlers were open range cattlemen, and their way of life was the prevailing one until property owners began fencing in the early 1880s. There were some incidents, and some fences were cut before the cattlemen realized the freebooting days were over and began buying and fencing land themselves. Longhorns were the original stock here, but herd improvement began early. Sheep and goats were introduced in the early 1880s, and cotton farming began about 1884. Farming and ranching are still important here, and the county has substantial oil and gas production, too.

Runnels County and the settlement that was chosen to be the county seat when the county was organized in 1880 both were named for Hiram G. Runnels. Hiram Runnels did not play a large role in Texas public affairs, but he was governor of Mississippi before he moved to Texas in 1842 at the age of 46. Runnels settled in Brazoria County, and he was a delegate

1

2

1) *Steelman Andrew Carnegie built 1700 libraries in cities and towns around the United States, in the early 1900s. The Carnegie Library in Ballinger was built in 1909. It was allowed to run down in the 1930s and there was some talk of tearing it down, but the people of Ballinger decided to restore it, and it apparently is going to be here for generations to come. The library is at 204 North 8th Street.*

2) *The Lynn-Hathaway Building at 800 Hutchins Street is another recorded landmark. This one, too, was built in 1909.*

3) *A bronze monument stands on the courthouse grounds in Ballinger as a memorial to Texas cowboys and to one cowboy in particular. Mr. and Mrs. Gus Noyes commissioned Pompeo Coppini to create the monument after their son Charles was killed. Young Noyes died in 1917 when his horse fell with him during a roundup on the family's ranch in Concho County.*

3

to the Convention of 1845 that ratified annexation and wrote the constitution for the new state of Texas. Runnels fought a duel with Volney E. Howard while he was in Mississippi. Howard was wounded but he survived and moved to Texas and had a county named for him.

The county seat here took the name Runnels City, and it was on its way to becoming a city. County officials had just completed a new jail when they began to hear rumors that a railroad was coming. A delegation from Runnels City visited with officials of the Gulf, Colorado and Santa Fe in 1885 and let them know they hoped the railroad would come through Runnels City. But the railroad's agents had a better idea. They paid a rancher $6,000 for a tract of land at the junction

1) The first post office in Runnels County was established in this log cabin at Blue Gap in 1878. The old post office is about 2 miles off Farm Road 1773 northeast of Winters.

2) Northeast of Winters off Farm Road 382 is the cabin where folk doctor Grandma Nancy Parker lived and dispensed her herb medicines in the late 1800s.

of Elm Creek and the Colorado River, a few miles south of Runnels City. The railroad created a new town on this site and made it the temporary terminus of its line. The new town was first called Hutchins City, but the name was later changed to Ballinger to honor railroad lawyer William Pitt Ballinger.

The Gulf, Colorado and Santa Fe spread ballyhoo around, suggesting that Ballinger would rival Fort Worth and Dallas. Special excursion trains were scheduled to carry people to the new town for a big land sale on June 29, 1886. The railroad offered free refreshments at the site, and anybody spending as much as $100 for land in Ballinger could get the price of his ticket refunded. It worked like a charm. The railroad took in more than $100,000 the first day of the sale. Free lots were then offered to any residents of Runnels City willing to relocate in Ballinger. Several residents did, and Ballinger was launched. Officials of the new town engineered an election on moving the county seat to Ballinger the same year. Residents of the county voted to keep the government at Runnels City. But people continued to move from Runnels City to Ballinger, and finally the government moved, too, in 1887. A courthouse was built in 1889. It is still in use. But it has been remodeled and enlarged.

A handsome statue of a cowboy and his horse stands on the courthouse grounds as a memorial to cowboys and to one cowboy in particular. The Noyes family had sculptor Pompeo Coppini create the monument after their son, Charles, was killed in an accident on a cattle roundup.

Buildings displaying historical markers here include the First Presbyterian Church at 301 Broadway, the old German

1) The Santa Fe Railroad created two new towns when it extended its line from Ballinger to San Angelo. The towns were Rowena and Miles. Joe Thiele thought the outlook for Miles was so rosy the place should have an opera house. Thiele opened one on the second floor of the bank building he built in Miles. A hotel on the opposite corner had a walkway extending over the street to the opera house during Miles' brief heyday.

2) Some of Miles' senior citizens meet every day in a room on the ground floor of the old Thiele Building to create quilts the way their mothers and grandmothers did it.

2

Methodist Church at 420 Strong and the Lynn-Hathaway Building at 800 Hutchins. The old Carnegie Library at 204 North 8th Street is a recorded National Landmark, and it is now being restored. Composer David Guion was born and raised in Ballinger. He is credited with composing *Home on the Range.*

The first post office built in Runnels County still stands near Winters, north of Ballinger. The Blue Gap Post Office was built of logs in 1878. Another cabin of the same period was occupied about the same time by Nancy Parker. She practiced folk medicine here in the frontier days, using teas and ointments made from herbs and weeds. Residents of this part of Runnels County were ministered to a few years later by the first woman to be licensed by a Texas medical school.

Bonnie Parker was born in Rowena. She moved to Dallas after her father died in 1914. Bonnie took up with outlaw Clyde Barrow in 1932. This photograph apparently was made sometime during a crime spree that lasted until lawmen ambushed Bonnie and Clyde in Louisiana and shot both of them to death. Bonnie is buried in the West Dallas Fishtrap Cemetery.

Dr. D. Emery Allen lived and practiced medicine in a town called Content in the 1890s and early 1900s. She later moved to Fort Worth, and everybody else in Content moved somewhere else. Content had the first cotton gin in Runnels County, but nothing is left of the town now except the cemetery, 16 miles northeast of Winters, off Farm Road 382.

The Gulf, Colorado and Santa Fe Railroad created two other new towns when it extended its tracks from Ballinger to San Angelo in 1888. These towns are Miles and Rowena. Charlsie Poe says in *Runnels Is My County* that a rancher named Jonathan Miles put up some of the land and money the railroad wanted as its price for extending the line, so Miles got to name the way stations. He named Miles for himself, and he named Rowena for the young woman Miles Junior mistakenly thought he was going to marry.

Bonnie Parker was born in Rowena in 1910. Her father was working as a bricklayer here at the time. He died when Bonnie was four, and the family moved to Dallas, where Bonnie was buried in 1934 after lawmen ambushed her and Clyde Barrow in Louisiana.

CONCHO COUNTY

The Concho River makes its connection with the Colorado in this county. The county was created in 1858 and named for the river. Mussel shells are found in the river bed, and the river is named for them. Concho is Spanish for shell. The river was known to the early Spanish explorers, and it was

1) The shells in the bed of the river here gave the early Spanish explorers the idea there might be pearls, too. The Spaniards called the river Concho. Concho is the Spanish word for shell.
2) Concho County was named for the river. There are shells, but no pearls.

known by a couple of other names before the name Concho stuck. The Spanish once had the notion there were pearls in the river. And they may have built their San Clemente Mission here at the junction of the Concho and the Colorado. There is an historical marker, 12 miles north of Millersview on Farm Road 2134. But there is also a marker at another site, in Runnels County. There is confusion about exactly where the mission was, because there is nothing left of it.

The attempt to maintain a mission lasted only a few months here in 1684 for the same reason that the Germans did not settle here in the 1840s. There were too many unfriendly Indians. The German syndicate Adelsverein bought the rights to this area from Henry Fisher and Burchard Miller.

The Fisher-Miller grant included 3 million acres between the Llano and the Colorado. The treaty John Meusebach made with the Comanches did not extend to this part of the grant. The first white settlers did not come here until about 1870.

A few cattlemen came before that. One of the first was John Chisum. He had established a big cattle operation in north Texas in the late 1850s. Chisum supplied beef to the Confederate armies during the Civil War, driving cattle to Confederate depots in Louisiana and Arkansas and the Indian Territory. He extended his operation to this area in 1862 or 1863. He sold out his north Texas interests at the end of the war, but he continued to run cattle here until he moved on to New Mexico about 1870. Chisum sent his cattle from here to

1

2

1) The town of Paint Rock was designated the county seat when Concho County was organized in 1879. The stone courthouse was built 7 years later. 2) The pioneer cattleman John Chisum extended his operations into what is now Concho County during the Civil War. Chisum started his cattle business in Denton County and became one of the Confederate Army's big meat suppliers during the war.

market in New Mexico and Colorado after the war ended. Charles Goodnight drove them for him, on the Goodnight-Loving Trail, for a dollar a head. Chisum was known as "Jinglebob John" because of the way he trimmed the ears of his cows to mark them as his. The cut he used left part of the ear dangling in what the cowboys called a "jinglebob." "Jinglebob John's" spread was northeast of the present town of Paint Rock, about ten miles east of U.S. 83. There is a marker on U.S. 83, about 4 miles north of Paint Rock.

Concho County was not actually organized until 1879, 19 years after the legislature created it. The town of Paint Rock has been the county seat from the beginning. The present courthouse was built in 1886. The town was founded about the time the county was organized, and it was named for the primitive art the Indians left on the rock cliffs beside the Concho River. There is an overhang here, creating a shelter the Indians obviously used for generations.

Concho County has some oil and gas, and there is some farming and some irrigation, but the biggest business still is ranching. The population of the county and the county seat has been declining since the 1930s. Eden is now the largest town and principal market in the county. Eden's situation, at the intersection of U.S. 87 and U.S. 83, is better than Paint Rock's. But Eden's population has been declining in recent years, too. Eden has nothing to do with Adam and Eve or serpents. It was named for Fred Eden. He opened the first store here about 1879.

1) Paint Rock took its name from some primitive art work left behind by the early Indian inhabitants of this area. The Indians used the shallow rock caves on the banks of the Concho River for shelter and they painted figures and symbols on the walls of the caves. These painted caves are listed in the National Register of Historic Places. *Some of the paintings were done more than a thousand years ago. Some are only a little over one hundred years old.*

2) The painted rocks are on private property, but visitors can get access or arrange guided tours through Chris Roach (Box 235, Paint Rock, 76866, 915-732-4242). Roach conducts the tours himself and he always wears a revolver when he visits the caves because he says he often sees rattlesnakes here.

2

McCULLOCH COUNTY

Two brothers named McCulloch came to Texas from Tennessee in 1835. Both of them fought many battles for Texas. Both of them became brigadier generals in the Confederate Army. One of them was killed in a Civil War battle. This county is named for that brother. He was Benjamin McCulloch. The other brother was named Henry. He survived the war and lived until 1895.

Ben McCulloch had charge of one of the "Twin Sisters" cannons at the Battle of San Jacinto. He fought with the Texas Rangers against the Indians and in the war with Mexico in 1845. He went to California during the gold rush, and he served briefly as sheriff of Sacramento County before he

McCulloch County was named for one of the heroes of the Battle of San Jacinto. Ben McCulloch also fought in the Mexican War and he was serving as a brigadier general in the Confederate Army when he was killed in 1862.

returned to Texas. McCulloch was serving as a U.S. marshal when the Texas Legislature created this county and named it for him in 1856. Ben and his brother, Henry, both were part of the Confederate force that persuaded the Union garrison at San Antonio to surrender when Texas seceded from the United States in 1861. Ben was killed in the Battle of Elk Horn in 1862. He is buried in the State Cemetery in Austin.

There was no rush to settle McCulloch County just because the legislature created it and gave it a name. The entire area was still full of buffalo and Comanches in 1856. There were not enough settlers here to need a county government until 1876. The government was organized in July of that year, and a settlement near the center of the county was chosen to be the county seat. The settlement was named Brady in honor of Peter Brady. He made one of the first surveys here. A chain of mountains and a creek here were named for him, too.

Sixty-two counties in Texas are still using courthouses built before 1900. This county is one of them. There has been some modernizing inside, but the outside of the courthouse at Brady still looks very much as it did when it was built in 1899. The old county jail built in 1909 at 117 North High Street, is a registered National Landmark.

The part of Texas most of us think of as central Texas is east of here, but the actual geographic center of Texas is here in northeast McCulloch County. There is a state marker near but not at the site. The marker is on U.S. 377 a little north of Placid.

Trail drivers moved their cattle trails to the west as farmers in the counties east of here put up more and more fences. The Western Trail was the principal route used between about 1876 and the arrival of the railroads. The Western Trail came up from the south through Brady, and it crossed the Brady Mountains at Cow Gap, according to the legend on the state

1) McCulloch County is one of the Texas counties still using a courthouse built in the 19th century. County officials in modernizing the interior have been careful to preserve the original appearance of the exterior.
2) The old McCulloch County Jail at 117 North High Street in Brady looks medieval, but it was built in 1909. It is being preserved and restored.

marker on U.S. 283, ten miles north of Brady. This trail crossed the Red River at Doan's Crossing and went on to Dodge City.

Brady got rail service fairly early, but there was no rail line south of here for a long time, and ranchers to the south walked their cattle to the railhead at Brady until 1930. There was a trail between here and Sonora, one hundred miles long, fenced on both sides.

The Texas Frontier Regiment established an outpost on the San Saba River here as part of the frontier security screen during the Civil War. A few ruins of Camp San Saba are visible at the site, about eleven miles south of Brady, off U.S. 87.

One of the episodes that made James Bowie famous on the frontier occurred near Calf Creek. Some of the details are set out on the historical marker eleven miles southwest of Brady, off Ranch Road 1311.

James Bowie and his brother, Rezin, were born in Tennessee. They moved to Louisiana in the early 1800s, and they speculated in land and smuggled slaves for a time. Jim Bowie was wounded in a fight during this period, and shortly after that fight he acquired the knife that became his trademark. It is not clear whether he made it or somebody else made it. One story is that his brother, Rezin, had it made for him. Anyway, it became the Bowie knife and part of the Bowie legend. It was a large knife with a heavy blade. Bowie was reputed to be very handy with it and very ready to use it. Jim Bowie came to Texas in 1828. He took Mexican citizenship and married a

1

2

1) Jim Bowie made part of his reputation here in what is now McCulloch County. Bowie and ten or eleven companions tangled near Calf Creek with a band of more than 150 Indians, and his side won, according to Bowie's account.

2) Waco claims to be the heart of Texas. But the center of Texas is here in McCulloch County.

3) The first Swede to settle in Texas probably was Swen Swenson. He encouraged other Swedes to move here. About 7000 immigrants came in from Sweden between 1848 and 1910. McCulloch County was one of the places they chose to settle. Ninety-five families established three small settlements near Brady. This marker recording their contributions stands near the East Sweden Cemetery, about 5 miles east of Brady.

3

Mexican woman. A few months after the wedding, Jim and his brother, Rezin, and about ten other men, got into a fight with Indians here at Calf Creek. There were 164 Indians. Bowie and his party killed 80 of the Indians. The rest gave up the fight after about 24 hours and ran away. This is according to the marker. The information apparently came from the report Jim Bowie made to the Mexican vice governor at San Antonio. Somebody else might have asked for a second opinion on the number of Indians. But Vice Governor Juan

The weathered ruins of the U. S. Army's old Fort McKavett on a hill in western Menard County look like what you might expect an abandoned frontier fort from the Indian days to look like. But Fort McKavett will not look like this much longer. The army left here in 1883. The roofs caved in and some of the walls fell down in the years after that. But Fort McKavett was far enough from any major settlements to escape the kind of scavenging that wiped out some of the old stone forts. Most of the stones are still here and the Texas Department of Parks and Wildlife is now restoring Fort McKavett. The restoration is incomplete, but the fort is open to visitors. It is south of U.S. 190, where Farm Roads 1674 and 864 meet.

Martin Veramendi was Mrs. Jim Bowie's daddy.

Jim Bowie's wife died about two years after this incident. Bowie was killed at the Alamo in 1836. His brother, Rezin, went back to Louisiana and went into politics.

MENARD COUNTY

Menard County includes the site of one of those forts the U.S. Army built to guard the frontier after Texas entered the Union. Fort McKavett was established on the upper San Saba River in 1852 while this area was still part of the vast District of Bexar. The fort was named for Captain Henry McKavett. He was one of the U.S. officers killed in the war with Mexico.

U.S. troops withdrew from Fort McKavett in 1859, and they did not return until after the end of the Civil War. Indians destroyed many of the fort buildings, but they were rebuilt and some new buildings were added after the troops returned in 1867. The buildings were built of native limestone and cypress from the banks of the Guadalupe River. Several

Menard County was named for the founder of the city of Galveston. Michel B. Menard was a French Canadian. He moved to Texas in 1832. He was one of the signers of the Texas Declaration of Independence. He probably was never in this part of the state. He died before the legislature created this county and gave it his name.

of the buildings are still standing. The troops left for the last time in 1883.

The fort is maintained now by the Texas Department of Parks and Wildlife as a state historic site. It is open to visitors, and there is no admission fee.

Menard County was created by the Texas Legislature in 1858 and named for one of the signers of the Texas Declaration of Independence. Michel B. Menard was born in Canada. He came to Texas first in 1829 as a fur trader. He came back to stay in 1832. Menard served in the Congress of the Republic of Texas. He founded the city of Galveston, and he died there two years before this county was established and named for him.

This was another case where conditions were not conducive to settlement until a number of years after the county was created. There were not enough settlers here to organize a county government until after the troops returned to Fort McKavett. The organization was completed in 1871. The town of Menard has been the county seat from the beginning, but the town was originally called Menardsville.

The county court met the first time under a live oak tree. The first courthouse was built in 1872. The present courthouse was built in 1931. The people of Menard County persuaded the Fort Worth-Rio Grande Railroad to extend its tracks from Brady in 1910 with inducements like free right-of-way and a free depot. The citizens shortened the name of the county seat to Menard when they completed the depot. Rail

1

2

1) The early settlers in Menard County built a canal to divert water to their farms along the south bank of the San Saba River. The canal flows through the town of Menard and across the courthouse lawn.

2) The old Menard depot on U.S. 83 is now a museum, open Saturday and Sunday afternoons.

3) The Country Store on U.S. 83 conducts a flea market in May. The rest of the year, the store offers local arts and crafts and homemade foods for sale.

3

service began in February of 1911. It ended in 1972. The depot is now a museum.

Irrigation began early in Menard County. The first irrigation canals started delivering water from the San Saba to farmlands around Menard in 1876. Farming is still important, and there is some oil and gas in the county, but ranching is the main business here.

The last remnant of the Dalton Gang was wiped out here in 1897 when Sheriff John Jones and five of his deputies caught up with Jim Crane and Jim and Jourd Nite. The officers shot Jourd Nite and Jim Crane to death and captured Jim Nite. Those three were reputed to be the last survivors of the outlaw band Bob and Emmett Dalton organized in 1891. Most of the gang was killed in 1892 while trying to rob a bank in Coffeyville, Kansas.

Spanish explorers probably visited this area as early as the middle 1500s. Coronado probably passed this way. The first attempt at settlement occurred in 1757. The Spanish established a mission on the San Saba just west of the present city of Menard. They called it San Sabá de la Santa Cruz, and they established a presidio on the opposite bank of the river to

A relic of the earliest Spanish attempt at settlement still stands here on the San Saba River just west of the town of Menard. This is what is left of the presidio the Spanish built to protect the Mission San Saba de la Santa Cruz. Indians burned the mission and kept the presidio more or less under siege until the Spaniards left in 1768. Stories persist that the Spanish had a gold mine near here. There is a cave on a ranch 12 miles northwest of Menard that the owner believes to have been a mine. But no gold has been found in it.

protect the mission. Part of the idea was to protect the Apaches from the Comanches, and part of the idea was to look for gold and silver. There may have been a little mining. There have been rumors of a lost gold mine ever since. But the effort to protect the Apaches from the Comanches was a complete failure. The Comanches killed two priests and burned the mission in 1758. The rest of the mission staff took refuge in the presidio and the garrison there held out for ten years. Persistent Indian attacks eventually forced the Spanish to leave the San Sabá Presidio. They moved south to the Mission San Lorenzo de la Santa Cruz in what is now Edwards County in 1768.

Indians used the old presidio as a camp ground. Cattlemen penned their herds inside the walls and used the presidio as an overnight camp in the days of the great cattle drives. The place was showing considerable wear by 1936 when part of it was restored. The ruined presidio is now a county park and open to visitors.

There was a big stone fort in Mason County in the frontier days, but it did not survive. Fort Mason was too handy to the town of Mason. The people of Mason helped themselves to the stone after the army abandoned the fort. The only building now standing at the site of old Fort Mason on a hill south of the courthouse is a replica.

MASON COUNTY

This county was settled a little earlier than Menard County because it was not quite as far from established settlements when it was created from part of Bexar and Gillespie counties in 1858. A few German settlers had moved into this area from Fredericksburg as early as 1848.

The U.S. Army established one of its frontier outposts beside a spring here in 1851. The post was named Fort Mason probably in honor of Lieutenant George Mason. The lieutenant lost his life in the war with Mexico. Federal troops left Fort Mason and all the other outposts on the Texas frontier when Texas seceded from the Union. Colonel Robert E. Lee was the commanding officer here at Fort Mason in 1861. He was summoned to Washington, and he left Fort Mason just ten days before Texans voted to leave the Union. Lee was still wearing the U.S. uniform when he left Texas because his native Virginia had not yet left the Union. President Lincoln wanted Lee to take command of the U.S. armies. But Virginia left the Union in April after the Southern attack on Fort Sumter made war inevitable. Robert E. Lee resigned from the U.S. Army two days later and took over command of the Army of Virginia.

Fort Mason was approximately in the center of the county when the county was created. The county and the county seat both took the name of the fort. The town of Mason developed from a trading post outside the fort. It was designated the county seat in 1861, shortly after the U.S. troops left. The vacant fort was a temptation to the settlers,

Many of the buildings in Mason are built of sandstone but all the sandstone did not come from the buildings at Fort Mason. Sandstone is a plentiful and popular building material in this area. The Classical Revival Mason County courthouse is made of it. This courthouse was built in 1909. It is listed in the National Register of Historic Places.

and much of the material used in buildings in the town was liberated from Fort Mason. Federal troops returned to the fort briefly after the Civil War, but it never was a major post again. The buildings were not rebuilt, and the scavenging continued after the troops left for the last time in 1869. There are no original buildings standing on the site. But there is a replica of one of the buildings where Fort Mason stood.

A large part of the town of Mason has been designated a National Historic District. The district includes the Courthouse Square, the old Reynolds-Seaquist Mansion and a number of other homes.

The Mason County Museum is in an old school house at 300 Moody Street. The school house is one of the buildings made of stone borrowed from the fort.

The Mason County War kept this area in some turmoil in 1875 and 1876. The history books call it the Mason County War or the Hoodoo War, but it was really a feud, and it started with a dispute over the ownership of cattle and the lynching of some suspected rustlers. Two groups formed, and ten or twelve men were killed in the ambushes and assassinations that followed until the feud died down.

The topaz is the official gem of Texas, and the best place to find topaz is west and northwest of Mason. But rockhounds should be sure to make arrangements with property owners before going prospecting. Most of the land here is in ranches. Cattle, sheep, goats and hogs are the chief money makers.

The German settlers in the Hill Country were not very sympathetic to the Confederate cause during the Civil War. One German settlement in southern Mason County changed its name to Loyal Valley after the war to make the point. Loyal Valley was the final home of John O. Meusebach. The founder of Fredericksburg moved here after he retired from running the Adelsverein settlement syndicate. He died here in 1897, and he was buried at Cherry Spring in Gillespie County.

1

1)The home known as the Grant-White house is another Mason landmark. It was built in the 1870s on State Highway 29 just east of downtown.

2) The Moran House is on the other side of Highway 29, a little farther east. It is sandstone with a limestone trim. Both these houses are private residences.

3) One of the most imposing buildings in the Mason Historic District is the house Thomas Broad built in 1887 on Broad Street. Edward Reynolds bought the house and enlarged it in about 1900 and it has been owned by the Seaquist family since 1919. There are 17 rooms and 14 fireplaces in this house. Tours can be arranged for a fee.

2

3

1

2

1) The Old Mason Grammar School building at 300 Moody Street was built of sandstone taken from the fort in 1887. The building now serves as a library and museum. The museum is open afternoons during the summer.

2) Rock and gem collectors are partial to Mason County. More topazes are found here than anywhere else in Texas. Some ranchers allow rockhounds on their property for a fee. The Nu-Way Drive-In Grocery on the west side of the square in Mason usually has information about these places.

3) The founder of Fredericksburg retired to a farm in southeast Mason County in 1869. John Meusebach developed a large orchard and rose garden on his place at Loyal Valley. His home is gone but the remains of Meusebach's rock bathtub are still here. Oldtimers said Meusebach had a grape arbor around the tub and a cistern to supply the water for his bath.

3

N. A. Taylor's book *"2,000 Miles in Texas on Horseback"* about his tour of Texas in 1877 recalls a visit to Loyal Valley. Taylor stopped at Meusebach's place. He describes it as a garden spot with 60 varieties of roses and several varieties of peaches, pears, apples, plums and grapes. The visit prompted Taylor to make some general observations on the differences between German settlers and American settlers on the frontier. He wrote that the Americans were loners and the Germans settled in groups. He said he found the Americans wasted little effort on making themselves comfortable because they wanted to be ready to move on if things didn't go to suit them. He said he found the Germans determined to make over whatever place they stopped until it suited them.

This ruin at Pontotac in the northeastern corner of Mason County is all that is left of a school founded in 1883. The San Fernando Academy failed after a few years and a public school operated in the old building until 1927. The building has been disintegrating since then.

KIMBLE COUNTY

The area that is now Kimble County was inhabited by Apaches when the first Spanish explorers came through here. The Spanish never made any attempt at settlement. The Apaches had been displaced by Comanches by the time Anglo settlement began in the 1850s. The first settler of record was Raleigh Gentry. He established a small farm on Bear Creek, about ten miles northwest of the present city of Junction. Gentry sold out in 1862 to Rance Moore. He apparently was the first cattle rancher. Louis Korn brought in the first sheep in the same year. Ranching is still the biggest business, and this county is one of the leaders in production of wool and mohair.

The early settlers had major problems with the Indians during the first twenty years. The last killings blamed on Indians here occurred in 1876. Outlaws were causing more problems than the Indians were by that time.

The legislature created Kimble County in 1858. But it was not actually organized until 1876. The first county seat was a little settlement called Kimbleville a short distance northeast of the present town of Junction. The county was placed in the judicial district presided over by Judge W. A. Blackburn of Burnet. Former Congressman O. C. Fisher says in his book *It Occurred in Kimble* that Judge Blackburn received word the outlaws were threatening to prevent any court meeting in Kimble County. The judge scheduled a session for April, 1877. He advised Major John B. Jones of the Texas Rangers Frontier Regiment that he wanted an escort, and he told the

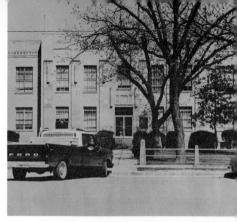

1

2

1) The Llano River is formed by the junction of the North Llano and South Llano at Junction. A dam at the U.S. 290 highway bridge forms a small lake and there is a city park here at the eastern edge of Junction, with picnic tables and barbecue grills and a public boat ramp.

2) The present Kimble County courthouse in Junction is the third courthouse building the county has had. The original courthouse was built in 1878. This one was built in 1929.

3) The Junction County Jail has proven more durable than the county's courthouses. The jail was built in 1892 and it is still in use. Gunslinger John Wesley Hardin's brother Gip was confined here in 1896 after he was accused of killing one of Junction's hotelkeepers.

3

major why. Fisher says Jones provided the escort. He also brought three companies of rangers into the county a few days before the court session. The rangers swept through the canyons of the North and South Llano rivers where the horse thieves, cattle rustlers and gunmen had their hideouts. Judge Blackburn arrived at the oak grove that served as the temporary court to find about 40 hoodlums chained to the trees. He handed out the sentences he thought were indicated, and the outlaw element had considerably less credibility in the new county after that.

The county seat was moved shortly after that first trial to a new location at the junction of the North and South Llano rivers. The new settlement was named Junction for its loca-

1) *Kimble County is a leading producer of wool and mohair. Shearers make good money here in the spring, moving their portable rigs from ranch to ranch and shearing the sheep and goats.*

2) *Angora goats were first brought to Texas in 1849. Texas has produced most of America's mohair since the 1920s. Seventy-five percent of all the Angora goats in the United States are concentrated in this part of Texas. These goats have just been shorn. The average adult Angora produces about 5 pounds of mohair. These same goats, before the shearers got to them, are pictured on page 79.*

1

2

tion. The first courthouse was built in 1878. That building burned a few years later, and all the county's early records went up in smoke. The present courthouse was built in 1929.

Kimble County was named for one of the heroes of the Alamo, but this is another one of those cases where the legislature changed the spelling of the name. The man the legislature meant to honor was George C. Kimbell. He and a few other citizens went from Gonzales to San Antonio on March 1, 1836 to reinforce Colonel Travis' little garrison there. Kimbell was killed with the others when the Mexicans stormed the Alamo on March 6th.

The Kimble County Historical Museum has a number of pioneer artifacts on display at 4th and Congress in Junction.

1
2

1) One of the recorded landmarks in Kimble County is the old Pepper home on U.S. 377 about 5 miles south of Junction. This was the first two-story house in Kimble County. It was built in 1877. Dr. R.H.P. Wright bought it in 1905 and Fay Wright Stevenson grew up here. She was the first wife of the late Governor Coke R. Stevenson.

2) Coke R. Stevenson was born in Kimble County in 1888. Stevenson held a number of public offices before he was elected governor in 1941. The only political race he ever lost was for the U.S. Senate. That was in 1948. Lyndon Johnson won that race by a narrow and disputed margin. Stevenson retired to his Kimble County ranch where he died in 1975 at the age of 87.

There is no admission fee, but the museum is not normally open except on Sunday afternoons during the summer months. Tours may be arranged at other times by appointment.

The Kimble County Library at 208 North 10th Street in Junction has a collection of the books and mementos of former Congressman Fisher. Junction is proud also of being the birthplace of the late former Governor Coke Stevenson. The house where the late Mrs. Stevenson grew up is one of the recorded landmarks here. The house is about five miles south of Junction on U.S. 377. It was built of limestone by B. F. Pepper in 1877. It was the first two-story house built in Kimble County. Mrs. Stevenson's father bought the place in 1905. He was Dr. R. H. P. Wright. The house has been in the Wright family ever since.

Some of the other old buildings with historical markers here are the Kimble County Jail at North 5th and Pecan, an old log cabin at North 3rd and Pecan, an old rock store building at 6th and College, and the old Cloud house, five miles east of town on Farm Road 2169.

Quarter horses race here in Junction in August during the annual Hill Country Race Meet and Goat Sale.

The scenery along U.S. 377 between Junction and Telegraph is worth seeing.

The highway department has made it easy to miss towns like Junction with freeways like Interstate 10. The freeway just skirts the edge of town. Out here beyond the billboards and the commuters, it is possible to see the beauty in the highway builders' art. Travelers from southeast Texas may find the open spaces between the vehicles on Interstate 10 the most inviting scenery here.

SCHLEICHER COUNTY

The South Concho River, Devil's River, and the San Saba flow through Schleicher County, but they don't flow a whole lot. The riverbeds are often dry between rains, and sometimes it is a long time between rains. So stockmen were not as quick to move in here as they were in some other areas. William Black was about the first one in 1876.

Schleicher County was created from part of Crockett County in 1887. But it was not organized until 1901. The county was named for Gustav Schleicher. Gustav was a German intellectual. He came to Texas in 1847 with a small group of other German intellectuals. They founded the communistic colony of Bettina on the Llano River near the present town of Castell. Gustav moved to San Antonio and got a job when the communistic experiment folded in 1848. He went on to become a member of the Texas legislature, an officer in the Confederate Army and a member of the U.S. House of Representatives before he died in 1879.

The town of Eldorado was chosen to be the county seat when the county government was organized here in 1901. The town had been founded by W. B. Simmiman, W. L. Gray and M. H. Murchison. They established a general store and then offered free lots on the adjacent land to anyone willing to settle here. The three founders chose the name of the town. It is not clear what their inspiration was. There was another one once, but this is now the only town in the county. The courthouse was built in 1923.

Eldorado has a woolen mill making fabrics from the wool and mohair produced in the area. Most of the land in the county is devoted to sheep and goat and cattle ranches. But

1

2

1) Eldorado is the only town in Schleicher County and it has been the county seat since the county was organized in 1901. The dignified limestone courthouse was built in 1923 after the original courthouse burned. Eldorado is Spanish, and the Spanish would pronounce it el-du-RAH-do. But the people here call their town el-du-RAY-duh.

2) The Schleicher County Museum on U.S. 190 opposite the courthouse is open on Mondays, Wednesdays and Thursdays. The museum is in an old stone building and the exhibits include furnishings and tools from the pioneer days. The name of this town is older than the town or the county. El Dorado or Eldorado is Spanish for "The Gilded." The earliest Spanish explorers heard and believed a story that somewhere in the New World there was a city so rich that its ruler wore only gold. The Spanish gave the name "El Dorado" to this mythical ruler and his mythical city. They spent a lot of time and energy searching for El Dorado. But this Eldorado is not the El Dorado they were looking for.

3) Stagecoaches continued to run through Eldorado after they had been replaced by trains in most other places. Light coaches like this ran between Sonora and San Angelo until 1915, following about the same route U.S. 277 follows through Eldorado.

3

1) *The old Schleicher County Jail building on the courthouse grounds has a homey appearance. It is plain from the outside that somebody lives here, besides the prisoners. The sheriff lives on the ground floor. This is still the case in a few other Texas counties and it once was the usual rule, but it will not be the rule here much longer. Schleicher County is building a new and modern jail on another part of the courthouse lawn.*

2) *The El Dorado Woolen Mill in the 400 block of Main Street in Eldorado buys wool from local ranchers and turns it into upholstery material for furniture factories in the East. The mill also produces limited quantities of wool blankets and a few clothing items for sale at the mill.*

3) *The Hill Country blends into the Plains here. U.S. 190 is the main road and the hills gradually level out as you travel westward on 190.*

3

the oil and gas wells now produce more money here. The county is popular with deer hunters.

The Schleicher County Museum has a collection of implements and furnishings used by the early settlers. The museum is on U.S. 190, just east of U.S. 277.

The railroads were a long time reaching this part of the world. The stage line between Sonora and San Angelo continued to operate up until about 1915. The coaches followed approximately the same route as the present U.S. 277. They changed horses at a stage stand ten miles south of Eldorado and at a stand 18 miles north of Eldorado. There are state historical markers at both locations.

Irion County is another county where a railroad rearranged the order of things. This county was created in 1889. The principal settlement in the county at the time was at the headquarters of the Sherwood Ranch. The settlement became the county seat and took the name of Sherwood. A typical Texas courthouse was built in Sherwood in 1900. It is standing here still . . . but the county government left in 1936.

IRION COUNTY

Spanish explorers were traveling through what is now Irion County as early as 1650. The stagecoaches on the run from San Antonio to San Diego and the Butterfield Overland line came through here between 1858 and the beginning of the Civil War. But few of the travelers found any reason to stay. The population of the county reached a peak of about 2,000 in 1940, and it has been declining since then.

Irion county was created from part of Tom Green County in 1889. It was named for Robert A. Irion. He was a doctor. He was born in Tennessee, and he lived in Mississippi before he came to Texas in 1832. Dr. Irion was commandant of Nacogdoches Municipality during the revolution. He served in the Senate of the Republic of Texas, and he was secretary of state during Sam Houston's first term as president. He died in 1861, 28 years before this county was created and named for him.

There was no real settlement here until after the Civil War. The principal settlement at the time the county was created was at the headquarters of the Granville Sherwood Ranch. This settlement was named Sherwood and designated the county seat when the county was organized. A stone courthouse was built in 1900. The Kansas City, Mexico and Orient Railroad put Sherwood out of business.

The railroad extended its line westward from San Angelo in 1910, and it did not stop at Sherwood. The railroad builders created a new town to be the first stop in Irion County. The new town was a short distance southwest of Sherwood. It was

1

2

1) The Kansas City, Mexico and Orient Railroad passed Sherwood by when it extended its line through Irion County in 1910. The railroad created a new town a few miles southwest of Sherwood and named it for railroad man M. L. Mertzon. The settlers and the government moved from Sherwood to Mertzon. The county built a new courthouse at Mertzon in 1937.

2) The Irion County Museum and Library in Mertzon is open Mondays, Tuesdays and Thursdays from 8 a.m. til noon. Mertzon is one of the smaller county seats in Texas. The population is just over 500.

3) Mertzon has only recently developed a city water system. Every household here had its own windmill before the system was developed and many of the private mills are still standing and still operating. Most of the land here is unsuitable for farming and there is not much rain, but there is some irrigation along the spring-fed Dove and Spring creeks.

3

named Mertzon for M. L. Mertzon. He was one of the directors of the railroad at the time. The railroad attracted settlers and business to Mertzon, and the county seat was moved from Sherwood to the newer town in 1936. The present courthouse was built in Mertzon in 1937. The old courthouse is still standing in what is left of Sherwood.

Oil was discovered here in 1928, and the income from the county's oilfields today is several times what the sheep and cattle ranches earn.

The Battle of Dove Creek is described in the section on Tom Green County. But this clash between the whites and the Kickapoo Indians may have occurred within the present boundaries of Irion County, about eight miles east of Mertzon, at or near the county line, in January, 1865.

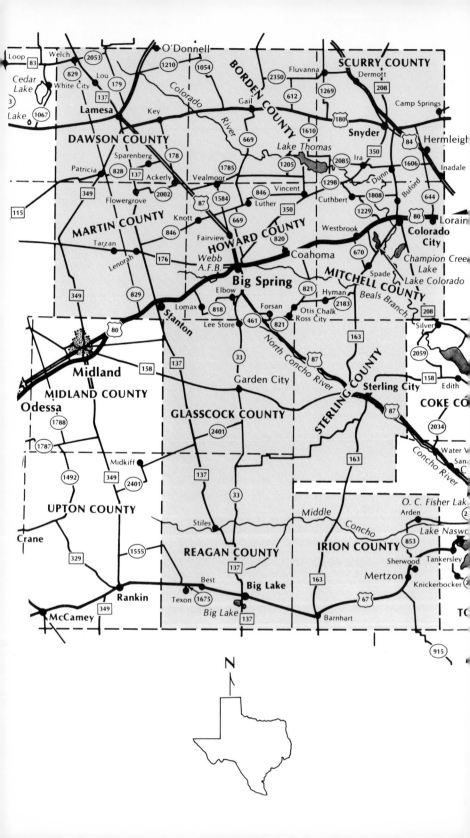

Big Spring area

Howard, Dawson, Borden, Scurry,
Mitchell, Sterling, Reagan, Glasscock and
Martin counties

The Republic of Texas mounted a campaign about 1840 to push the Comanches out of West Texas. The Comanches quickly learned to avoid contact with groups of rangers or soldiers. They began to specialize in quick raids on isolated ranches and settlements and wagon trains instead. They became very bold during the Civil War years when the frontier forts were mostly closed down. They actually pushed the frontier back during the war.

Troops returned to the frontier forts after the end of the war, and white hunters moved onto the grassy plains here to slaughter the buffalo. Hundreds of thousands of the animals were killed for their hides. The carcasses were left to rot. White settlers made a little pocket money in the 1880s by gathering up the weathered bones and shipping them to Eastern fertilizer plants on the new railroad.

The presence of the soldiers and the elimination of the buffalo helped to force the Indians onto reservations. Cattlemen moved onto the plains here in the 1870s, and settlers followed in the 1880s.

They found there was more water than people had thought, in springs and underground. The settlers said when the underground water was found that they should have expected there'd be something valuable under the ground because there

1

1) *A big spring gave the city of Big Spring its name and its start. The spring is no more, but the city is doing fine. The Indians made regular stops at the big spring in what is now Howard County long before the first whites came here. The spring has quit flowing, but the city of Big Spring has turned the site into a park. There is water and a swimming pool. But the water is being pumped in. The Comanche Trail Park at the spring site includes a large recreation area and a golf course and a number of campsites. There is no fee for camping here.*

2) *Randolph Marcy stopped at the big spring when he was exploring routes across West Texas in 1849. Marcy was a captain in the U.S. Army. He rose to brigadier general during the Civil War and served as chief of staff for his son-in-law, General George B. McClellan. But Marcy spent most of his career on the frontier. He spent six years in Texas and he wrote 3 books about his experiences:* Prairie Traveler, Thirty Years of Army Life on the Border *and* Border Reminiscences.

2

was so little on top. But they didn't begin to realize the value of the underground resources until the first oil well was drilled in 1920 in what was to become known as the Permian Basin. The Basin extends from here into southwestern New Mexico. It holds some of the richest oil and gas deposits known to man.

HOWARD COUNTY

People were attracted to the area that is now Howard County before the beginning of recorded history. The attraction was a spring. The spring water attracted animals, and the animals and the water attracted people. The buffalo and the Indians were using the spring when the Spanish first became aware of it about 1768. It is not clear when it first began to be

1) Howard County was named for Volney E. Howard. He once lost a duel with the man Runnels County was named for.

2) The first railroad in West Texas naturally made Big Spring a stopping point. The locomotives of that day were driven by steam. They had to have a lot of water and Big Spring had plenty. The first railroad was the Texas and Pacific. The T&P built its maintenance shops for this section of the line in Big Spring and the T&P still has a big switching yard here.

called Big Spring.

Captain Randolph B. Marcy of the U.S. Army put the spring on the map in 1849. The gold rush was drawing great numbers of people to California from the eastern states. Captain Marcy and his troopers escorted a wagon train from Fort Smith, Arkansas, to Santa Fe. They crossed Texas through the Panhandle. But Marcy and his men explored a different route back to Fort Smith. They swung down into Texas to about where the city of Pecos is today and then turned northeast toward Colbert's Ferry on the Red River. They passed approximately through the sites of the present cities of Odessa, Midland, Big Spring and Snyder.

The first permanent settler did not come here until 1870. He settled at Moss Spring a few miles southeast of Big Spring. Cattlemen followed and grazed their herds on the open prairies here until fencing began. Pioneer rancher C. C. Slaughter based part of his vast operation here from sometime in the 1870s through the 1890s. Slaughter called his outfit the Long S. He was one of the first cattlemen to import prize bulls to improve the Texas herds. He was at one time the biggest taxpayer in Texas, with 55,000 head of cattle grazing on one million acres of land.

1

2

1) A few of the early settlers here came to help build the railroad and then stayed to help build Big Spring. The city has been the county seat since Howard County was organized. The county government began operations in a rented house. The first courthouse was built in 1883. The present courthouse was built in 1952.

2) One of the men the T&P brought to Big Spring built the city's first fine house. Joseph Potton and his wife were born in England. They came to Texas in 1881. Potton started working for the T&P in Marshall and transferred to Big Spring in 1891. The Pottons built this home about 1901 and it remained in the Potton family until the Big Spring Tourist Development Council bought it in 1975. It is furnished with antiques and open to visitors daily except Monday. The address is 200 Gregg Street.

The legislature created Howard County in 1876 from parts of Bexar and Young counties. The county was named for Volney Erskine Howard. He was a complete believer in moving westward. Howard was born in Maine in 1809. He moved to Mississippi in 1832 and went into politics. He fought a duel there with Hiram G. Runnels and lost. Howard survived and moved on to Texas. Runnels did, too. Runnels stayed. Howard served in the Texas Legislature and represented Texas in the U.S. Congress before he made his final move on to California in the 1850s.

Howard County was not actually organized until 1882. There was a little settlement by then at the big spring. It was a buffalo hunters' camp with a hotel, a wagon yard, eight saloons, several huts and a few tents. But Big Spring was on its way to becoming a city. The same abundant water that drew the animals and the Indians and the settlers attracted the attention of the Texas and Pacific Railroad. Jay Gould had the T&P tracks laid through here in 1881. The T&P built elaborate shops in Big Spring. The shops brought in new settlers. And the railroad brought Big Spring its most unusual settler.

The Earl of Aylesford came here from England looking for a place to hunt and settle down. The earl had been a close friend and companion of King Edward VII when the king was

1

1) *The Finch Building at 121 Main Street is the oldest building in Big Spring. It was originally a butcher shop, built by an English earl.*
2) *His lordship also owned the Cosmopolitan Hotel at 123 East 3rd Street. This old photo of the Cosmopolitan is from the files of the BIG SPRING HERALD. The earl died here in 1885 during a drinking spree. The hotel is gone. A store stands on the site, now.*

2

Prince of Wales. He had a fair amount of cash and a huge collection of valuable guns. The earl met Jay Gould somewhere and Gould suggested that he check out Big Spring. The nobleman arrived in Big Spring sometime in 1883. He bought some property and built a ranch house. He bought and sold a hotel and a saloon, and he built the first stone building in the town. The earl drank too much. One visitor said there was a pile of empty bottles outside the earl's ranch house as big as a haystack. But he was very generous and very popular, and the residents of Big Spring mourned when he died in January of 1885 at the age of 36. It was understood that the earl and his countess had divorced. They had two daughters and no sons, so the title and the estate would have to pass to the earl's brother. The earl supposedly came to Texas to build a new fortune he could leave to his daughters. He gave a big party for Christmas 1884 and never recovered from it.

1

2

1) The tallest building in Big Spring is the Settles Hotel built by oilman W. R. Settles in 1930. It was the showplace of West Texas. The Settles closed in 1980.

2) Symphony concerts, ballet programs and plays are presented regularly in the picturesque Big Spring Municipal Auditorium.

3) The Record Shop in the 200 block of Main Street in Big Spring is a favorite with record collectors. This was the original record shop in this area. Owner Oscar Glickman still has a big stock of 78s he got stuck with when the LPs came out. Oscar is very tolerant of other peoples' taste. He recalls when the cowboys out here thought he was corrupting their children when he sold them classics.

4) The Heritage Museum at 510 Scurry Street has a collection of antiques and old photographs and pioneer artifacts.

4

3

1) The Heritage Museum has the world's biggest collection of Henry W. Caylor paintings. Caylor lived and worked in Big Spring for 40 years. Many of his western scenes like this were commissioned by wealthy ranchers, so he made a comfortable living from his art. Caylor died in 1932 but his reputation is still growing.

2) The biggest general store in this part of the west operated in this building for many years. Joseph Fisher came to Big Spring in 1881 and started a little store in a tent. Fisher's brother William joined him in 1883. Their J&W Fisher Company was soon bringing in merchandise from Fort Worth by the carload to supply the expanding ranches. The Fisher Company occupied this building from 1884 until it went out of business in 1941.

Big Spring has been the county seat here since Howard County was organized. The present courthouse was built in 1952. Cattle ranching is still important here. Cotton is the principal farm product. But oil is the biggest factor in the economy of Howard County now. Several boom towns sprang up briefly southeast of Big Spring when the first well in the Howard Glasscock Field was completed in 1925.

The big spring that gave the city its name is now surrounded by the Big Spring City Park. It is on the southern edge of the city off U.S. 87 and Farm Road 700. It is free, and there is a free campground.

The Big Spring State Park is also on the southern edge of the city, off Farm Road 700. This is not a large park, and there are no provisions for camping. There is a dance pavilion, and there are picnic tables. The chief attraction is the scenic drive overlooking the city. There is an admission fee.

The Heritage Museum at 510 Scurry features art and displays dealing with the history of the area. There is no admission fee.

One Big Spring home is listed in the *National Register of*

1

2

1) *A marker on U.S. 87 at Farm Road 821 testifies that the first commercial oil well in Howard County was completed here in 1925. Howard County has been a major oil producer ever since.*

2) *Two or three boom towns sprang up in southeast Howard County as more successful oil wells were drilled in the 1920s. Five thousand people lived in the boomtown of Chalk at one time. But they didn't stay. The wells are still producing here, but no trace is left of the town of Chalk.*

3) *Many of the big refineries in the United States are now processing imported crude. But there is still enough local oil to keep the Cosden-Fina Refinery at Big Spring busy. The refinery was built by Josh Cosden in 1929. It is owned now by American Petrofina.*

4) *An isolated peak in the oil field in southeast Howard County has been called Signal Mountain since pioneer days. This was one of the peaks the Indians used for their smoke signals.*

4

3

1

1) Playing dominoes is serious business in Big Spring. The World Championship Texas Style Domino Tournament is held here each year. The tournament lasts for three days and there are substantial prizes. Warming up for the next tournament begins as soon as a tournament ends. 2) The windmills came to these plains in the late 1880s. Many of the windmills were replaced by electric pumps in the 1950s and 60s when electricity was cheap. But people are not taking many windmills down, now. There is plenty of wind and it costs nothing.

2

Historic Places. It is the Potton-Hayden house at 2nd and Gregg streets.

The Department of Defense closed the Webb Air Force Base here in 1977, and the city has been developing the former base as an industrial park.

DAWSON COUNTY

The county is named Dawson, and there is a town here named Klondike. You might think this area was settled by Canadians or by Robert W. Service. It was not.

The little town of Klondike apparently was named by the early settlers in the middle 1890s for the gold rush area in the Yukon Territory. But the county was named for a Texas hero. The legislature created this county in 1876 and named it for Nicholas Mosby Dawson. He was a veteran of the Battle of San Jacinto, and he was killed by Mexican soldiers outside San Antonio in 1842. Dawson was living in Fayette County in September of that year when General Adrian Woll brought an army up from Mexico and captured San Antonio. Dawson organized a company of volunteers to go to San Antonio to fight the invaders. The Mexicans ambushed Dawson's company east of San Antonio. Dawson and thirty-four other Tex-

1) Lamesa is the banking and business center of Dawson County. The city also has several small industries and a population of about 12,000. Lamesa has been the county seat since Dawson County was organized in 1905. The present courthouse was built in 1916.

2) There was a time when most of the paved streets in Texas were paved with bricks. That was in the time when most streets in Texas were not paved. Most of the original brick paving has been covered with asphalt in most cities, now. But the bricks are still bare in Lamesa.

ans were killed in the fighting that followed. The fight is referred to in the Texas history books as the Dawson Massacre because there is some evidence some of the Texans were trying to surrender when they were killed. The remains of Dawson and his men were buried with honors in a vault on Monument Hill at LaGrange. General Woll and his Mexicans withdrew from San Antonio September 20th, and returned to Mexico.

The Mexican government issued a colonization grant to Dr. John Cameron in 1827 authorizing him to settle people in the area that is now Dawson County. But the area was full of buffalo and Indians.

Dr. Cameron got into the history books by taking part in the seige that forced the Mexicans to leave the Alamo in 1835, and he accomplished some other things. But he never brought any settlers here. White buffalo hunters moved in during the 1870s, though, and the cattlemen followed. Most of the land was tied up in grazing leases until the early 1900s. Land began becoming available to settlers then, and the settlers sometimes waited in line at Big Spring for weeks to claim it.

Dawson County was not formally organized until 1905. There was a contest for the county seat between a settlement named Chicago and a settlement named Lamesa. Chicago was older. It started in 1877 as the headquarters for W. C. Bishop's ranch. Bishop came from Chicago. But the county's voters picked Lamesa to be the county seat, and Chicago folded up. The people there moved to Lamesa. The present courthouse was built in 1916. Lamesa is Spanish for "the

1

2
3

1) The oldest three-story house in Lamesa is now the county museum and art center. This place was built in 1917 by Ulyss Dalmont. He was one of the pioneer ranchers in Dawson County.

2) Displays in the museum include antique furnishings and the work of some local artists. The museum is normally open only on Sunday afternoons, but tours can be arranged at other times. The museum is at Avenue M and South 2nd Street, but the mailing address is 404 21st Place, Lamesa, 79331.

3) The Hardy Morgan Ranch is one of the registered landmarks here. Morgan was one of the earliest ranchers in the county. He built this house on State Highway 137 south of Lamesa in 1905. It plainly has been altered since.

table'' and the name refers to the flat tableland the town sits on. The Spanish would make it two words, "La Mesa." And they would pronounce it Lah-MAY-suh. A few visitors pronounce it that way, but the people here call their town La-MEE-suh.

The Dawson County Museum is in an old home at 2nd Street and Avenue M, in Lamesa. It features antique furnishings and displays dealing with the county's history. The museum is normally open only on Sunday afternoons, but tours can be arranged at other times.

There are state historical markers here on the M. D. Lind-

Farms were generally smaller in this part of the state before farmers started using underground water for irrigation. Most of the crops now are raised on very large tracts of land that may include several old farmsteads. This is why you often see, here, abandoned farmhouses surrounded by big mechanized farms. The previous owners may have died broke or they may have struck oil and moved to the city. Much of the mechanized farming today is done on leased land by people who live somewhere else.

sey house at 602 South Bryan, and on the Hardy Morgan ranch house, 12 miles south of Lamesa on State Highway 137. These are private residences.

Nearly 50,000 acres of farmland in Dawson County is irrigated. Cotton is the leading crop, and Dawson County is one of the leading cotton counties in the state. But the oil and gas fields earn about twice as much money as all the farm and ranch products together.

BORDEN COUNTY

Borden County was late being settled, but it is named for an early Texas settler. Gail Borden Jr. arrived in Texas in 1829. He was born in New York in 1801. He had lived in Indiana and Mississippi before he moved to Texas. Borden was one of the busier men on the frontier. He was a surveyor for the Stephen F. Austin colony. He founded the *Telegraph and Texas Register* at San Felipe in 1835 and published it there and in Harrisburg and Columbia and Houston before he sold it in 1837. Borden helped lay out the city of Houston. He was agent for the Galveston City Company, and he was a trustee of the Baptist society that founded Baylor University.

Borden invented a dried meat biscuit in 1849. He moved to New York to try to market that product. It never caught on, but he discovered a process for condensing milk in a vacuum in 1853. His first two or three attempts to market that product failed, too. But the Union army started buying condensed milk on a big scale when the Civil War began. That launched the Borden Milk Company.

Gail Borden established a meat packing plant in Colorado

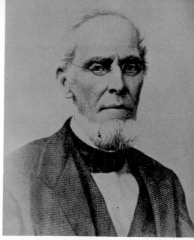

1

2

3

1) He never lived in this area, but the founder of the Borden Milk Company once lived in Texas. Gail Borden was a prominent citizen in the days of the revolution and the Republic, long before Borden's trademark was born.
2) Borden published one of Texas' earliest newspapers, but he moved to the North before the Civil War. The first big customer for his evaporated milk was the Union Army. Borden died nearly twenty years before the legislature created this county and gave it his name.
3) The town of Gail was also named for Gail Borden. Gail is the county seat.

County after the end of the Civil War, and he maintained a summer home there from 1871 until he died in 1874.

No one lived here except Indians and a few buffalo hunters when the legislature created this county and named it for Borden in 1876. There were no settlements. The county had a population of only 35 in 1880.

The population was 222 when the county government was organized in 1891. A place near the center of the county was designated the county seat, and the little settlement that

1

2

1) The Borden County government operated in a schoolhouse when the county was first organized. A frame courthouse was built in Gail in the early 1890s and it served until 1939 when the present brick building was built. Only about 200 people live in Gail, now. In 1920, the population was 1500 and there were 3 hotels.

2) The Borden County Jail is an antique. The jail was built in 1896. The stone walls are two feet thick. It is no longer used and the sheriff now has to take his prisoners to the next county, whenever he has prisoners.

developed was named Gail for the same man the county was named for. This was ranching country at the time, and it still is. There were some contests between ranchers and farmers when the public lands became available to be claimed in 1902. Cowboys and farmers fought several battles for places in the claim line. Some farmers succeeded in claiming land, and some of them stayed. But some others were wiped out by droughts. Many Borden County landowners have been made rich by oil and gas in more recent times.

The southeastern edge of the Llano Estacado is in western Borden County. This is also called the Staked Plain. The edge of it is often called the Cap Rock. It is a high mesa extending up into the Panhandle and over into New Mexico. It is part of the Great Plain that extends all the way into Canada. The plain rises abruptly from the surrounding terrain. There are places on the New Mexico side of it where the rise is so steep horses cannot climb it. The cliffs there resemble a stockade, and this may be the reason the early explorers called it Llano Estacado. They may also have given it this name because they had to drive stakes in the ground to make a trail they could find on the way back. There were no trees here then. Llano

1) The Borden County Museum on Main Street has a collection of furnishings, tools and implements used by the early settlers. The museum is open Sunday afternoons.

2) The Staked Plain or Llano Estacado begins here in Borden County. The edge of this high mesa is usually called the Cap Rock. The road from Gail to Post climbs the Cap Rock. It is Farm Road 669.

1

2

Estacado is Spanish for "Staked Plain." The term cap rock actually refers to a very hard layer of soil, like rock, that lies just under the surface of the high mesa, rather than to the plain itself, or the edge of the plain. The isolated section of the Staked Plain just south of the town of Gail was formed by erosion. The name of it is Mucha-Kooga Peak, but it is usually called Mushaway Peak. Farm Road 669 offers some good views as it climbs up the edge of the plain, north of Gail.

Gail is one of our smaller county seats. You can see it all from U.S. 180. The population hovers around 200. There is a county museum with collections of pictures, furnishings and clothing from pioneer days. It is open normally only on Sunday afternoons. The courthouse here was built in 1939.

There are provisions for camping, fishing and water sports at several resorts around Lake J. B. Thomas. The lake is on the Colorado River in the southeast corner of Borden County, extending into the northwest corner of Scurry County. Access is by Farm Road 1610 and Farm Road 1205, south of U.S. 180.

No county in any state in the United States produces more oil than Scurry County. This well is pumpng alongside a commemorative marker the state put up when total production in the county passed one billion barrels. That was in 1973.

SCURRY COUNTY

If you owned some land in Scurry County, you wouldn't worry about oil prices going up, if you owned the mineral rights, too. The entire county is not an oil field. But the oil fields in this county are some of the most productive in the country. Scurry County produces more oil than any other single county in the United States. The first well was completed here in 1923. There was a little ceremony in 1973 marking the production of the one-billionth barrel. They put up a marker on U.S. 84, six miles north of Snyder, to help future generations understand the role this county played in the Age of Petroleum.

Scurry County was created in 1876. The legislature was carving up the old original District of Bexar that year, and many of the counties in this part of the state date from 1876. But this was another case where there were too few residents to justify any formal organization in 1876. Scurry County did not get its own government until 1884. The town of Snyder has been the county seat since that date. The present courthouse was built in 1909 and remodeled in 1972.

Scurry County was named for William Redi Scurry. He was a hero of the Civil War. Scurry came to Texas from Tennessee in 1840. He practiced law and served in the Congress of the Republic and published a newspaper briefly in Austin. Scurry served as a major in the war with Mexico, and he was commisioned a brigadier general in the Confederate Army in 1862. He was mortally wounded in a battle with Union troops in 1864, but he refused to allow himself to be moved from the battlefield until his troops had won the battle. That was the

1

2

1) Scurry County was named for Confederate hero William R. Scurry.
2) The Scurry County courthouse in Snyder was built in 1909 and remodeled
in 1972. The white buffalo statue commemorates the killing of an albino buf-
falo near here.

Battle of Jenkins' Ferry on April 30, 1864. Scurry died shortly
after it ended. He is buried in the State Cemetery in Austin.

The town of Snyder grew up around a trading post W. H.
Snyder established here in 1877. He bought merchandise in
Dallas and hauled it out here in wagons and sold it to the buffalo hunters. Some of the hunters built shanties and dugouts
near the trading post so Snyder laid out a town site in 1882.
There was some farming, but ranching was the principal occupation here before the oil was discovered.

The first railroad reached Snyder in 1908. The railroad was
the Roscoe, Snyder and Pacific. It is still in business, but it
doesn't go anywhere near the Pacific, and it never did. The
R.S.&P. tracks never reached beyond Fluvanna, in the
northwestern corner of Scurry County. The railroad operates
now only between Roscoe and Snyder. The offices are in
Roscoe, in Nolan County. The line has two engines and
several hundred boxcars. Its main business is shuttling boxcars between the Missouri-Pacific tracks at Roscoe and the
Santa Fe tracks at Snyder. It is one of the shortest railroads in
the country, and it is reputed to be one of the most profitable.

Snyder has two museums. The Scurry County Museum is
on the grounds of Western Texas College on State Highway
350 South. It has exhibits dealing with the pioneer days and
with the development of the oil and cattle industries. This
museum is open weekdays and Sunday afternoons, and there
is no charge for admission. The Diamond M Foundation
Museum is also free. It is in the Diamond M Building at 907
25th Street. It features a collection of paintings and sculpture
by several famous artists.

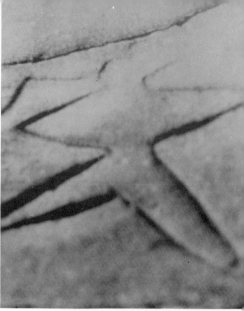

1

2

1) *The Scurry County Museum is on the campus of Western Texas College on State Highway 350, south of Snyder. Exhibits include relics of the Indian and Pioneer days.*

2) *The Indian exhibits in the museum include photographs of carvings found on the walls of Sandstone Canyon in eastern Scurry County. The carvings themselves have been almost destroyed by erosion.*

3) *Buildings in Snyder displaying historical markers include the Grayum house at 2300 32nd Street.*

4) *The Diamond M Museum at 907 25th Street has some fine paintings and sculpture collected by the late C. T. McLaughlin. The museum is open Mondays through Fridays and it is free. McLaughlin was a prominent Scurry County rancher and oilman.*

4

3

1   2

1) An old steam engine donated by the Roscoe, Snyder and Pacific Railway is on display in Snyder's Towle Park. The little railroad is still in business. And this railroad's business is very good. Most of the shipments of fresh fruits and vegetables from California to the East Coast pass through its hands.

2) Towle Park has a small lake, picnic area and swimming pool and there is a prairie dog park where the little rodents that used to plague the ranchers so now entertain tourists.

3) A marker on State Highway 350 southwest of Ira recalls that the Indians killed one of President William Harrison's kinsmen here in 1849. The young officer was with Captain Marcy's expedition and he apparently made the mistake of thinking he could make friends with the Indians.

3

Several historical markers on the courthouse grounds detail some of the history of the area, and there is a statue of a white buffalo on the courthouse grounds because an albino buffalo was killed near here once in the days of the great buffalo hunts.

There are historical markers on the First Baptist Church at 27th and Avenue Q, on the First Christian Church at 2701 37th, on the First Methodist Church at 27th and Avenue R, on the First Presbyterian Church at 2706 Avenue R, on the First State Bank building at 2501 Avenue S, on the Dodson house at 3007 Avenue S, on the Clark house at 2306 32nd Street, and on the Grayum house at 2300 32nd Street. The houses listed are private residences and not open to the public.

The city's Towle Memorial Park has provisions for picnicking and swimming, and there is a prairie dog town in the park. Towle Memorial Park is on State Highway 350 South.

The first big boomtown in West Texas was Colorado City in Mitchell County. A few of the men enriched by the boom built a hotel in 1885 that was the finest place between Fort Worth and El Paso. The St. James Hotel had already passed its heyday when this picture was made. The boom in Colorado City was waning by 1886.

Pioneer cotton farmer Clemens Von Roeder developed several special types of cotton for this area. He developed a plant with a long staple and big boll, and he produced several strains that resist hail and wind and rust damage. The Von Roeder Cotton Breeding Farms are on U.S. 180, 3 miles west of Snyder.

MITCHELL COUNTY

Mitchell is another one of the counties created from the old District of Bexar in 1876. It was populated at the time only by Indians and buffalo and a few white buffalo hunters. There were only about 100 settlers in the county in 1880 when the Texas and Pacific Railroad let it be known that the T&P line from Fort Worth to El Paso would come through here. Business picked up right away. The first store in what was to become Colorado City was built that year. The first train arrived in 1881. Colorado City became the main shipping point for the ranches in this entire area. Colorado City became the county seat when Mitchell County was formally organized in 1881, and the town was booming by 1882.

Colorado City had a population of 10,000 by 1884. There were 28 saloons by then, and four hotels and four theaters, and it was being claimed that there were more millionaires in Colorado City than in all the rest of Texas together. Winfield Scott and some of the other big men in the area formed a corporation to build a fancy hotel. They called it the St. James. It was three stories, and it had every convenience that could be had on the frontier when it was completed in 1885. The proud owners held a grand opening party. They imported orchestras from Fort Worth and St. Louis and invited cattlemen from all over Texas and New Mexico. Colorado City was the only real town between El Paso and Weatherford, at that time. Some historians have called it the "Mother of West Texas."

1

2

1) *It was the T&P Railroad that put Colorado City on the map. The line reached here in 1881 on its way from Fort Worth to Sierra Blanca. The wire that fenced the ranges was unloaded here.*

2) *There are a couple of acceptable pronunciations of the name of the state of Colorado, but neither one works here. The people of Colorado City call their town Colo-RAY-duh City. The present courthouse was built in 1924.*

3) *The original Colorado City Opera House did not survive, but the second opera house is still here. This building was built in 1900. Colorado City Playhouse presents live productions here several times a year. The Opera House is on Walnut, behind the Post Office.*

3

   Colorado City was probably the first real boom town in West Texas. But the boom did not last long. Drought and a severe winter in 1885-1886 killed off and scattered the herds on the open range. The surviving ranchers began fencing in 1886. There was some recovery. But another severe drought began in 1892, and it lasted for two years. This one forced many ranchers into bankruptcy. Businessmen closed up and moved away. The population of Colorado City dropped to about 1,500. The city government even folded up.

   Colorado City had been incorporated in 1883. Bonds were voted and sold during the boom years for a sewer system and a city hall building. But no provision was made for redeeming the bonds. No financial records were kept, and the improvements were not built. The citizens decided that the best thing to do was to dissolve the corporation, and they did that in 1897. New bonds were issued to the holders of the old bonds when Colorado City was re-incorporated in 1907. The city recovered slowly from the disastrous drought of 1892-1894, but other railroads had reached into the area by

1) A preservation group is now restoring one of the homes built at the height of the first boom in Colorado City. This home was built in 1883 by J. P. Hodgson. It was bought the following year by rancher Winfield Scott and it was the Scott home until 1898. The address is 425 Chestnut.

2) One of Scott's early partners built this house at 605 Chestnut Street. The builder was Sug Robertson but the place is known as the Arnett home because D. N. Arnett bought it from Robertson in 1912. It has been in the Arnett family ever since. It is a private residence.

1

2

then and other shipping centers had developed. Colorado City's trade area was substantially smaller than it had been during the initial boom.

Most of the land here is in ranches still. But there is also substantial farming. The first bale of cotton in Mitchell County was grown in 1888. Cotton and feed grains are the main crops today. But the oil and gas wells produce the most money.

The first well in the Permian Basin was completed here in Mitchell County on the 25th of June, 1920. It was in the Westbrook Field, and there is an historical marker one mile west of Westbrook off Interstate Highway 20. The early oil production in the Permian Basin was from shallow wells. The presence of more oil, deeper down, was established by the 1930s, but there was little economic incentive for drilling deep wells until World War II increased the demand for oil. The

1

2

*1) Some of the equipment and furnishings that were in the T&P depot when it
was operating are on display, now, in the Colorado City Museum. A number
of other relics from the early days are on display here, too. The Museum is
east of the courthouse at 175 West 3rd Street. There is no admission fee.
2) Lake Colorado City State Park off Farm Road 2836, south of Colorado
City has provisions for fishing and swimming, camping and picnicking. This
is one of the state's Class I parks. There is the usual admission fee of $2 per
vehicle unless you have a season pass or a Senior Citizens' Passport.*

Permian Basin was once an inland sea. This is the eastern
edge of it. It stretches into New Mexico.

Colorado City takes its name from its location on the Colorado River. The county was named for Asa and Eli Mitchell.
They were brothers. The Mitchells came to Texas in the 1820s
and settled at the mouth of the Brazos River. Eli fought in the
Battle of Gonzales and Asa fought at the Battle of San Jacinto. The present Mitchell County Courthouse in Colorado City
was built in 1924.

Some furnishings and tools and photographs from the early
days are on display in the Colorado City Museum at 175 West
3rd Street. The museum is open daily except Monday, and
there is no charge for admission.

There are historical markers on the All Saints Episcopal
Church, 304 Locust Street, the First Baptist Church at 3rd
and Chestnut, the First Methodist Church at 333 Chestnut,
the First Presbyterian Church at 5th and Chestnut, the Colorado Opera House at 337 Walnut, the Arnett house at 605
Chestnut, the Coleman house at 175 West 3rd, the Hardegree
house at 305 Hickory, the Burns house at 304 4th Street and
on the Majors house at 425 Chestnut Street. The houses are
private residences and not open to the public.

There are provisions for fishing, swimming, picnicking
and camping at the Lake Colorado City State Park on the
lake, a few miles southwest of town. There is a fee for admission to the park.

1) A mountain near Loraine in northeastern Mitchell County is named for the Kiowa chief Lone Wolf. Some of the chief's tribesmen, including one of the chief's sons, were killed in a fight with Texas Rangers near here in 1874. Lone Wolf and some of his other braves came down from the reservation in Oklahoma to recover the bodies. The rangers got on their trail, but Lone Wolf eluded them after hastily burying his dead tribesmen.
2) Lone Wolf Peak may have been the burial place, but it is not certain.

STERLING COUNTY

This county and the county seat and the creek he lived on here all were named for W. S. Sterling. He was an Indian fighter and buffalo hunter and rancher. Sterling is believed to have had a camp on Sterling Creek as early as 1858. It is certain he was here and hunting buffalo in the early 1860s.

Sterling moved on to Arizona in 1881. He was serving as a United States marshal there when a band of Apaches ambushed him and killed him. The county that was named for him was created from part of Tom Green County in 1891.

The settlement that became the county seat had originally been called Montvale. The name was changed to Sterling City when the county was organized and named. Sterling City is on the North Concho River, about halfway between San Angelo and Big Spring. The U.S. Army established an outpost near here in 1853. It was about nine miles northwest of where Sterling City is today. There is nothing at the site today except a state marker. The presence of troops in the area made it possible for cattlemen to move their herds in here to take advantage of the free grass fairly early. The era of the open range lasted until about 1890. Settlers started fencing then, and sheepherders began moving into the area about the same time.

Sheep and cattle produce most of the agricultural income here still. But the agricultural income is less than half what

1

2

3

1) Some of the Spanish explorers probably passed this way earlier, but Anglos paid little attention to this area until the middle 1800s. The U.S. Army maintained an outpost and hospital here for about 12 years beginning in 1874. The camp may actually have been established in the 1850s, according to the marker at the site, on U.S. 87, about 9 miles northwest of Sterling City.
2) The first actual settler was a buffalo hunter named Sterling. He moved on farther west before this county was established in 1891, but the legislature gave it his name and the county seat took his name, too. The present Sterling County courthouse was built in Sterling City in 1938.
3) The county jail is much older and still in use. This is a quiet town. The population is under 1000.

the county's oil and gas wells earn.

The population of Sterling City reached 900 in 1914. It is under 800 now.

There are historical markers here on the R. P. Brown home on 4th Avenue, one block north of U.S. 87, and on the grave of the county's first physician, Dr. P. D. Coulson, in the Montvale Cemetery, on U.S. 87, four miles east of Sterling

1

2

1) The Gulf, Colorado and Santa Fe Railroad extended its line from San Angelo into Sterling City in 1910. The population increased a little, then, but it started declining in the 1930s. There never was a real boom here. The last passenger train left the Sterling City Depot a long time ago.

2) A few landowners raise crops with the help of expensive sprinkler systems, but most of them raise sheep and cattle. A number of them have additional income from oil royalties.

City, and at the site of Camp Elizabeth, on U.S. 87, nine miles northwest of Sterling City.

This is another one of those areas where the outlaws Jesse and Frank James reputedly did some of their hiding out. They are supposed to have raised some horses and done a little buffalo hunting from a hideout near Sterling Creek. If Jesse and Frank actually hid out in as many places as they are supposed to have hidden out in, they would have had little time to do the other things outlaws do.

REAGAN COUNTY

The event that put the University of Texas in the oil business occurred here in Reagan County in May of 1923. A syndicate of oil speculators brought in a well 14 miles west of the town of Big Lake on property leased from the University. The University owns more than 2 million acres, and wells on these lands have earned hundreds of millions of dollars for the University and Texas A&M since 1923. *The Reagan County Story,* published by the Reagan County Historical Survey Committee, says this discovery well was named Santa Rita #1 at the insistence of two Catholic women from New York. They invested money in the venture, and they believed the saint's name would bring good luck. Santa Rita is the saint of the impossible.

There is one story that luck dictated the site of Santa Rita #1. The driller's equipment broke down, according to this story, and he drilled where he did because he could not get his rig to the site where he meant to drill. *The Handbook of Texas* says this story is not true. The drilling site was selected

1

1) About one third of the land in Reagan County is owned by the University of Texas and the University's first oilwell was drilled here. There are several large ranches but very little farming. The average rainfall is only about 14 inches a year.

2) Reagan County was named for the first chairman of the Texas Railroad Commission. John H. Reagan came to Texas in 1839 and he held a variety of public offices from county judge to United States Senator. Governor Hogg named him chairman when the Railroad Commission was established. He retired from the office the same year this county was created. When Reagan died in 1905, the entire membership of the Texas legislature attended the funeral services.

2

by a geologist, according to the Handbook.

There was an element of luck in the University's ownership of this particular land. The Congress of the Republic set aside 231,000 acres of land to help support the University when the Congress decided in 1839 to create such a school. That land was sold, and some of the money was diverted to other purposes. The legislature decided in 1858 to appropriate more lands for the University on a schedule tied to the grants made to railroad companies. Every time the state granted a section of land to a railroad to encourage the building of rail lines, an adjoining section was reserved for the state. The decision of 1858 provided that one out of every ten sections reserved for the state would become the property of the University. The school would have accumulated more than 3 million acres of land in various parts of the state under this arrangement. The

1

2

1) *The first ranch house built in Reagan County was built by John E. Gardner in 1885. It is still standing on Ranch Road 1676 near Big Lake.*

2) *The original courthouse for Reagan County was built in a settlement called Stiles. This town was the county seat until 1925. The government moved that year to the newer town of Big Lake. It was one of those cases where the first railroad in the county missed the county seat. What is left of the original courthouse is still standing in what is left of Stiles.*

3) *The present courthouse in Big Lake was built in 1925.*

3

legislature decided in 1876 that it had been too generous. The land grants tied to the railroad grants were canceled. The legislature granted the University 1 million acres of land in West Texas, instead. That West Texas land was not thought at the time to be very desirable. But it was on that land that the Santa Rita #1 was drilled. Part of the Santa Rita rig was moved to the campus of the University of Texas in Austin years later, and it is still on display there as a reminder of the event that started the University on its way to becoming one of the richest schools anywhere.

Reagan County was created and organized in 1903 from part of Tom Green County. It was named for John H. Reagan. He came to Texas in 1839, and he held a variety of public offices before he died in 1905. Reagan was a member of the legislature, and he represented Texas in the U.S. Congress before the Civil War. He was postmaster general and then treasurer of the Confederacy during the Civil War, and he served a little time in prison for that before he was restored to citizenship. Reagan was elected to Congress again in 1875, and he moved up to the U.S. Senate in 1887. Governor Jim Hogg made him the first chairman of the Texas Railroad

1) The antique jail from the old town of Stiles is on display in the Reagan County Park at Big Lake.
2) There is also a replica of the Santa Rita #1 oil rig here, and provisions for camping, with trailer hookups.
3) The principal stagecoach route across West Texas came through this area. There was a rest stop at Grierson Spring near the present town of Best. It was also an army outpost. Little is left of them now, but there were some stone buildings here in the 1870s and 80s. Grierson Spring was connected to Fort Concho at San Angelo by telegraph. All the frontier forts had telegraph connections by 1876.

Commission when the Commission was established in 1891.

This area was explored by the Spanish as early as 1650. They and the Indians knew about the natural lake in the south central part of what is now Reagan County. This is a depression that collects and holds rainwater. It became a regular stop for people traveling between Fort Concho and Fort Stockton. This water hole has been called the big lake for longer than anyone can remember. So the town that developed here when the railroad came through was named Big Lake. It is the county seat now.

The county seat was originally put at a settlement called Stiles when the county was organized. A rancher named W. G. Stiles settled on Centralia Draw in 1890. Other settlers followed. Their settlement was close to the center of the county when the boundary lines were drawn. One of the settlers offered to donate a site for a town. So the settlement at Stiles was designated to be the seat of the government. A stone courthouse was built in 1911. But Stiles never grew much, and it went into a decline when the Kansas City, Mexico and Orient Railroad laid its tracks through Big Lake to the south. The people moved to the railroad. The government followed

Glasscock County was not on any major stage line in the stagecoach days and it has no freeway today. There was an oil boom here in the 1920s. There is substantial oil production, now, but the boom passed quickly. The population never has been much above 1200 and it is a little below that now. There is some farming in Glasscock County but most of the land is in ranches.

in 1925. The old stone courthouse still stands at Stiles, but little else is left of the former county seat. The Kansas City, Mexico and Orient was absorbed into the Santa Fe system long ago.

There was an army outpost in a canyon near the present town of Best, west of Big Lake. There was a natural spring. The army built some stone buildings and rock cisterns to hold the spring water. Grierson Spring was a substantial outpost and stage station from about 1875 to 1885. But much of the stone has since been borrowed for other buildings.

The oldest building still standing in the county is the John E. Gardner ranch house on Ranch Road 1676, southwest of Big Lake. It is a stone house with just one room, built in 1885. Gardner was a sheep rancher and county commissioner.

There are provisions for picnicking and camping in the large county park out Utah Avenue north of Big Lake. The park has trailer hookups.

GLASSCOCK COUNTY

Glasscock County was named for the same man the city of Georgetown was named for. Georgetown was named for George W. Glasscock because he donated the land for the original townsite in Williamson County. It is not clear which of his accomplishments prompted the legislature to name this county for him when it was created in 1887, nearly twenty years after Glasscock died. It may have been his interest in getting West Texas farmers to grow wheat. Glasscock is said to have built the first flour mill in West Texas as part of that effort.

1) It has moved once and changed its name twice, but Garden City has been the county seat since Glasscock County was organized in 1893. Garden City was developed originally by land speculators. The present Glasscock County courthouse was built in 1910.

2) This building was the courthouse for Glasscock County before 1910. It has been the county jail since then. The county is now building a new jail.

Glasscock was born in Kentucky. He lived in Missouri and Illinois before he moved to Texas in 1834. He had a business partnership briefly with Abraham Lincoln in Illinois. They operated a flat boat on the Sangamon River. Glasscock settled first in East Texas at Zavalla. He later lived at Bastrop and Austin. He was a member of the little Texas army that forced Mexican troops to give up the Alamo in December of 1835.

Glasscock County was formed from part of Tom Green County. The formal organization was not completed until 1893. The town of Garden City was designated the county seat at that time, and it has been the county seat ever since. The town actually was established originally at another site, about two and a half miles from the present site. The name was changed to New California and back to Garden City again before it became the county seat. The present courthouse was built in 1909.

There was a modest land rush here in 1908 when the state began making land available to homesteaders, and Garden City enjoyed a small boom between 1908 and about 1910. But the population of Garden City today is only about 300, and there are only about 1,100 people in the entire county. They are well behaved. The county jail has been vacant for years at a time.

There is some irrigation here and farms in Glasscock County produce crops of cotton and grain sorghum. But ranching is bigger than farming here, and oil is bigger than farming and ranching together.

MUSTANG SPRING

WATERING PLACE KNOWN AS EARLY AS 1849 WHEN CAPTAIN RANDOLPH B. MARCY OF THE U. S. ARMY STOPPED HERE EN ROUTE FROM FORT SMITH, ARKANSAS, TO EL PASO · DESCRIBED IN 1859 AS "MUSTANG POND, TWO MILES NORTH OF EMIGRANT'S ROAD" FIRST WATER WEST OF BIG SPRING

1   2

1) The most important thing for travelers to know in the early days in the west was where the water was. The reason Randolph Marcy explored this area in 1849 was to find a passable route across West Texas with enough water holes to keep wagon trains going. One of the water holes he charted was Mustang Spring between the present towns of Big Spring and Midland. 2) Pioneer rancher C. C. Slaughter had one of his headquarters camps at Mustang Spring when he was running cattle here in the 1880s.

MARTIN COUNTY

The area that is now Martin County is a long way from the principal German settlements in Texas. But the first settlers here were Germans. Cattlemen were grazing their livestock on the open range here earlier. And cattle baron C. C. Slaughter had a headquarters camp at Mustang Spring, north of the present town of Stanton. But there were no settlements when the Texas and Pacific Railroad laid its tracks through here in 1881. The railroad established a way station where the town of Stanton is now. The town was originally called Grelton.

Railroad officials persuaded some German settlers to move here from Kansas. Adam Konz organized the migration and established the first town. He and the other settlers were German Catholics. They did away with the name the railroad had given the place and named the settlement Mariensfield in honor of the Virgin Mary. The Catholic church they built was the first one in northwest Texas that did not begin as a mission.

The settlers established a school in 1882, and they got a post office in 1883. Martin County had been created by the legislature in 1876, but it was not formally organized until 1884. Mariensfield was designated the county seat. The present courthouse was built in 1975.

There were a few problems with Slaughter's Long S cowboys when the German settlers began fencing their property. But the real problem was a drought in 1886. Some of the settlers gave up and left. New settlers moved into the area after the drought, and they began raising cotton and feed

1) Stanton had a couple of other names before it became Stanton. Officials of the T&P Railroad decided in 1881 that there ought to be a town here. The railroad persuaded some German Catholics to move here from Kansas. The Germans changed the name from Grelton to Mariensfield. They built a church and monastery. The monastery building survives, but it is now private property.

2) A wave of Protestant settlers came in from the North in 1889, and they changed the name of the town to Stanton. The present courthouse was built in 1975.

3) The old county jail building has been turned into a museum. It is on the courthouse grounds.

crops. These crops were better suited to the climate than the wheat, barley and rye the Germans had favored. Most of the new settlers were Protestants. They changed the name of the town from Mariensfield to Stanton in 1889. The new name apparently was chosen to honor Edwin M. Stanton. He was Abraham Lincoln's secretary of war, so we can assume that most of the new settlers came from northern states.

Large crops of cotton and feed grains are being grown here still, but the oil and gas wells produce more income now.

The Martin County Historical Museum in the old jail building on the square has some pioneer furnishings and tools and old barbed wire. The original sheriff's office and an old cell block are also preserved here. There is no admission fee, but the museum is normally open only on Sunday afternoons.

Another historic building is the Kelly home at 201 East Carpenter. This house is the only building left of the Convent and Academy of Our Lady of Mercy, established by the Carmelite Monastery in 1882.

Martin County was created from part of the old Bexar District. It was named for Wylie Martin. He never was here, and he died more than 30 years before this county was

1) *The Martin County Historical Museum at 200 Broadway has one of the early model Eclipse windmills.*

2) *One of the historic homes in Martin County is the Milhollon Ranch house, built in 1907, on U.S. 80 about a half mile east of Stanton.*

3) *The horned toad is on the growing list of endangered species. But there is no shortage of the toads in this part of Texas. This reptile is called a horned frog in Fort Worth, where it is the mascot of Texas Christian University.*

created. Martin came to Texas in 1823 as one of Stephen F. Austin's colonists. He was active in public affairs, but he was lukewarm on the revolution. Martin thought the Declaration of Independence was premature, but he joined the Texas Army anyway. He was given command of a small detachment assigned to guard the Brazos River crossing at Richmond in April of 1836. He resigned after his men failed to prevent Santa Anna from crossing the Brazos. *The Handbook of Texas* says Martin complained that he was given too few men to do the job.

Wylie Martin later was chief justice of Fort Bend County, and he served one term in the Senate of the Republic of Texas.

The big event in Stanton is the Old Settlers' Reunion they've been holding for more than forty years. It is the second Saturday in July.

Texans speak of this kind of weather as threatening. But threatening weather is the most promising kind in this part of Texas. Sudden summer storms like this can cause flash flooding, but they also provide most of the rain the area gets. Some counties here average less than 12 inches of rain a year.

153

Midland-Odessa area

Midland, Upton, Crane, Ward, Loving,
Winkler, Andrews, Gaines and Ector
counties

This is the heart of the Permian Basin. The area also includes the southern end of the Llano Estacado. This area was famous for fine livestock before it became famous for oil. The livestock and the oil both are very important still.

The part of Texas known as the Permian Basin looks nothing like a basin. The geological formation that gives the area its name is underground today. The surface elevation is 2,000 to 3,000 feet. But this area was once covered with sea water. Changes in the earth's surface turned it into an inland sea. The basin formed then trapped the decaying remains of plants and animals and started the development of the oil and gas deposits that have made the area rich since they were discovered in the 1920s.

This area apparently was a tropical forest in more recent times. Bone fragments found here indicate that there were miniature horses and elephants and some form of human life here then. That was 18,000 to 20,000 years ago. But the area was grassy plain and semi-desert when Captain Randolph Marcy of the U.S. Army brought his troops through here in 1849. Bands of Comanches and herds of buffalo roamed the area then. The great war trail the Comanches used in traveling

Midland is a smaller Houston, a relatively young town with a slick and modern look. The economy is also similar, based mostly on petroleum, petro-chemicals and agriculture.

between the Panhandle of Texas and northern Mexico came through here. But Captain Marcy said the trail he blazed from the Pecos River to north central Texas would be a good route for a transcontinental railroad. The Texas and Pacific, thirty years later, adopted his recommendation.

MIDLAND COUNTY

Midland is near the center of the Permian Basin. Midland and Odessa are the centers of the business and industry generated by the oil and gas discoveries in the basin area. Oil was not discovered in Midland County, itself, until 1945, but refineries, pipelines and chemical plants have kept Midland booming since the late 1930s. Midland is a city of handsome business buildings, comfortable homes and considerable culture.

This was all public land and open range before the 1880s. The Indians and the buffalo had it to themselves except for an occasional stagecoach or wagon train. White buffalo hunters and cattlemen moved into the area in the years following the Civil War. But there were no real settlements before the Texas and Pacific Railroad laid tracks through here for the line from Fort Worth that was to link up with the Southern Pacific at Sierra Blanca. The railroad established a water stop and called it Midway, because it was about halfway between Fort Worth and El Paso. That was in 1881.

John Howard Griffin recalls in his *Land of the High Sky* that the first permanent settler did not arrive here until the following year. Herman Garrett was raising sheep in California when he heard stories about the country the T&P was

1

2

1) *Midland was a frontier village with mud streets wide enough to turn a wagon around in less than 100 years ago. It was the T&P railroad that first drew people here.*

2) *Midland's streets are still wide but everything else has changed since the 1890s. The city has been in a boom almost continuously since oil was discovered in the Permian Basin.*

3) *The finest place to stay in Midland during the first oil boom in the 20s and 30s was the Scharbauer Hotel. The Scharbauers were early settlers here. John Scharbauer came out from New York State in the 1880s. His brother Christian joined him in 1889, and they developed a prosperous ranching empire that became more prosperous when oil was discovered on some of their ranches. Christian Scharbauer's son Clarence built the Scharbauer Hotel in 1927. It was dynamited in 1973 to make way for a new Hilton.*

4) *The Midland County Courthouse is not as new as it looks. It was built in 1938 and modernized in 1974.*

3

4

n

1

2

1) The Midland County Historical Museum is in the basement of the county library building at 302 W. Missouri. It is open every day except Sunday.
2) The library has a replica of the skull found on the Scharbauer Ranch in 1953. This is the oldest human bone found so far in North America. This discovery has always been known as Midland Man, but the skull probably is that of a woman.

opening up in West Texas. Garrett put his sheep on a Southern Pacific freight train and shipped them to El Paso. The S. P. line ended there at the time. The T&P had not completed its link-up. Garrett and his sheep walked northeastward and met the T&P tracks and followed them to a likely looking spot a little northeast of the present city of Midland. The spot had looked likely to uncounted generations before. Garrett settled in Mustang Draw where Mustang Spring provided a reliable water supply. Captain Randolph Marcy had stopped at the same spot in 1849 when he was blazing a new trail back to Fort Smith after escorting an emigrant train to Santa Fe. It was on the Comanche War Trail. It had been an Indian campground for probably thousands of years. Carbon tests have proven that some human bones found near here in 1953 are 18,000 years old. Some archaeologists believe these remains are the oldest yet found in North America. The remains are in a vault at Southern Methodist University in Dallas. There are reproductions on display at the Midland County Library.

Settlers were drawn to the railroad and a few permanent houses had been built by 1884 in the settlement that was still called Midway. Several other towns were being called Midway. The post office complained about the duplications. So the name of this Midway was changed to Midland. The legislature separated the area from Tom Green County in 1885 and created a new county with the same name as the set-

1

1) *The original bell from the Alamo is on display at the Haley Library and History Center at 1805 W. Indiana in Midland.*

2) *The Haley Center also has a fine collection of authentic photographs of life on the range the way it really was.*

3) *The Museum of the Southwest has a collection of art on display in an old mansion at 1705 W. Missouri. It is free.*

4) *The Permian Basin Petroleum Museum at 1500 I-20 West has some elaborate exhibits dealing with history and science. There is an admission fee.*

3

2

4

1) Every house in Midland had its own windmill in earlier days. A few of the residents still have their own windmills and water tanks.
2) But Midland has developed a central water system supplied by water from the Colorado River and by deep wells. The city says it has enough water under ranches it owns to supply Midland's needs for more than 100 years.

tlement. The present Midland County Courthouse in Midland was built in 1938 and remodeled in 1974.

A cattleman from Chicago managed to buy a quarter of a million acres of land here in 1881. But most of the land in what is now Midland County continued to be held by the state until the middle 1890s. There were the usual contests between newcomers and the established ranchers when the land became available to be claimed. Then came the fences and a few farmers. Farming and ranching both got a big boost when the residents of Midland County discovered the windmill during the drought of 1886-87. Farmers could grow crops they couldn't grow before. Ranchers could put the water where their cows were instead of having to get the cows to the water. The citizens of the city of Midland originally had drawn their water from the few city wells. Individual windmills were a big improvement. Nearly every household had its own mill by 1888, and Midland was being called Windmill City. Midland later developed a municipal water system drawing its supply from wells drilled into formations oil prospectors had unintentionally discovered.

Midland County was mostly cattle country until the oil was discovered. John Scharbauer came here in 1887 to start a sheep ranch. He started running cattle in 1888, and he was the first rancher to bring registered Herefords to this area. His move encouraged other ranchers to begin improving the longhorn that had been the mainstay of the cow business on the plains before that time. Scharbauer was one of the earliest bankers in Midland. The Scharbauer family built the Scharbauer Hotel during the oil boom of the 1920s.

Many of the oil operators in the Permian Basin went broke

1

2

1) The oldest house still standing in Midland County is the place known as the Brown-Dorsev home at 213 N. Weatherford. It is open to visitors on Sunday afternoons and other times by appointment.
2) The Scharbauer home at 802 S. Main also has a historical marker. The Scharbauers first raised sheep and then went into the cattle business. They were among the first ranchers here to raise registered cattle.

during the early thirties. The Great Depression was only part of the problem for them. The big East Texas Oilfield had been discovered, and the state was wallowing in oil. Prices dropped to 10¢ a barrel. Some producers in this part of the state just stopped producing. But bonuses they had received from oil leases helped some of the ranchers survive.

The second oil boom in Midland is still in progress. It started in the late 1930s. Proration and conservation measures and the new demand created by the preparations for World War II raised the price of crude to 65¢ a barrel. Deeper wells were drilled. The Permian Basin became one of the great oil and gas producing areas of the world.

Midland County has more than 12,000 acres of irrigated farmland producing mostly cotton and grain. The income from ranching is about double that from farming. The income from the oil and gas fields is more than ten times the income from farming and ranching together.

Exhibits in the Permian Basin Petroleum Museum, Library and Hall of Fame trace the history of the Permian Basin and the development of the oil and gas industry in this area.

A display at the Midland-Odessa Air Terminal recalls some of the very early days of aviation. It is a restored flying machine built in Midland between 1909 and 1912. The builder was John Valentine Pliska. He was a blacksmith from Austria. He got caught up in the excitement generated by the Wright Brothers' flight at Kitty Hawk. Pliska had never seen a plane before he and a friend designed and built this one. They flew it a few times, but it was grounded in 1912 after a disappointing performance at an Independence Day celebration.

The blacksmith's airplane. John Pliska of Midland got so excited about what the Wright brothers were doing in the early 1900s that he designed and built a plane of his own. It flew a little bit, but Pliska got discouraged and grounded it after the spectators at an air show he staged in 1912 demanded their money back. Pliska's plane is on display at the Midland-Odessa Airport.

UPTON COUNTY

This was part of the open range up until the 1890s. Some of the wagon trains passed through here on the way to California as early as 1849 and 1850. The trail between Big Spring and the Pecos River crossings passed through Castle Gap in the hills in the west part of what is now Upton County. There is a marker in the county park near the gap recalling that this pass was also used by the Indians for centuries before the white man came.

There were only a few sheep and cattle ranchers here before 1890. One of the earliest settlers was Dr. George Elliott. He built the first house in the county in 1880 near what was to become the settlement of Upland. The legislature created Upton County in 1887 from part of Tom Green County. Upland was near the center of the new county, and it was designated the county seat when the county was organized formally in 1910.

The first railroad to reach the county was the Panhandle and Santa Fe. It passed well south of Upland. A man named F. E. Rankin donated some land for a new town on the railroad, and people started moving from Upland to Rankin.

1

1) *Some of the forty-niners passed this way. The wagon trains followed the paths of least resistance. When they had to cross a range, they looked for the lowest point. Many travelers came through this pass in western Upton County. They called it Castle Gap because the hill on the left reminded some early traveler of a castle in the old country. The traffic that came through Castle Gap was headed for the Horsehead Crossing on the Pecos River. There is a small park and picnic area in the gap. The access road is north of McCamey, off U.S. 385.*

2) *The original county seat of Upton County is now a sheep ranch. There was a town here, once. It was called Upland, and this was the courthouse. The stage line came through here, then, but the site is well off the road, now, and on private property a few miles north of Rankin.*

2

The government moved to Rankin in 1921. Upland has disappeared from the map.

The present Upton County Courthouse in Rankin was built in 1926 and remodeled in 1958. The legislature named this county for two Confederate soldiers. They were brothers and both were colonels in Hood's Texas Brigade. The Upton brothers were born in Tennessee. John was the older. He moved to California in the early days of the gold rush.

John's brother, William, and their mother moved to Texas in 1859 and acquired a farm in Fayette County. John moved from California to join them. Both brothers took up arms for the Confederacy at the outset of the war. John was killed at the Second Battle of Manassas in 1862. William survived to become a prominent merchant in Schulenburg, where he lived until 1887.

There is a free museum in the lobby of the old Yates Hotel, at 200 W. 5th Street in Rankin. It is open weekday afternoons.

There are no large towns in Upton County, but McCamey is about twice as large as Rankin. McCamey is southwest of Rankin on U.S. 67 and the Santa Fe rail line. But the railroad

1

2

1) The Upton County government moved from Upland to Rankin in 1921 and built this courthouse in 1926. This is not the standard Texas arrangement. There is no town square in the usual sense. The courthouse sits on a hill a little removed from the main part of town.

2) Some of this area's history is depicted in exhibits in the old Yates Hotel beside the railroad tracks in Rankin. The hotel was a busy place when the passenger trains stopped here but it has been closed for a long time.

3) The old McCamey railroad depot is being incorporated into the Mendoza Trail Museum on U.S. 67 in east McCamey. The Mendoza Trail Museum is named for one of the early Texas explorers. Juan Dominguez de Mendoza came this way in 1684. There is a free public campground in Santa Fe Park next door to the Mendoza Trail Museum.

3

did not create McCamey. Oil did. There was nothing here before 1920. A wildcatter named McCamey brought in a well near the tracks that year, and people swarmed in. There were 10,000 people here within a few months. Many of them lived in tents. At the height of the boom water was selling in McCamey for $1 a barrel. That was a good bit more than oil was worth, then. There were other successful wells and the area is still producing a lot of oil, but the leasehounds and speculators moved on to other boom towns after a short time. The population was down to 3,000 by 1950. It is about 2,500 now.

The Mendoza Trail Museum on U.S. 67 East in McCamey has a collection of furnishings and artifacts from the frontier days on display. The museum includes a ranch house built originally in Pecos County about 1900 and moved here later. It is open weekday afternoons except Mondays, and there is no charge for admission.

1) There is a huge monument on the southeastern edge of McCamey to an idea that must have seemed like a good one at the time. Oilmen were drawing oil out of the ground faster than it could be hauled away, here, in the 1920s. Some of the engineers thought they could create lakes of oil. They did not have the earth-moving equipment they have today, but they put men and mules to work gouging out big holes in the ground. The sides were banked and the whole thing was lined with concrete. This one covers an area of 8 acres. It was supposed to hold a million barrels of oil. But it never was filled. It leaked too much.

2) The original McCamey town jail has been on display at Burleson and 5th Street in downtown McCamey since the Chamber of Commerce fixed up old 5th Street for the town's 50th birthday in 1977.

2

Oil fields around McCamey were producing so much oil by 1928 that the producers had no place to put it all. Pipelines were being laid, and metal storage tanks were being built as fast as the construction methods of the day allowed. It wasn't fast enough. So oil company engineers decided to try something that had been tried in one or two other oil fields. They dug a big hole in the ground and banked dirt around the edges and lined the inside with concrete. It took several hundred workers four months to complete the job. The bowl was designed to hold 1,000,000 barrels of crude. A huge lid was made of wood to float on top. A system of lightning rods was installed around the rim to keep down the fire hazard during thunderstorms. The thing cost $250,000, but it never really worked. The weight of the oil cracked the concrete liner long before the bowl was filled. The cracks allowed oil to seep into the ground at a rate up to 500 barrels a day. The experiment was abandoned after less than two years. But the great pit is

An unmarked county road that runs across the top of King Mountain provides some nice views of this area. The scenic road branches left off Ranch Road 2463, where the concrete cross is, about two miles north of U.S. 67, east of McCamey. This road links up with U.S. 385.

still here sprawled over eight acres like a giant stadium. Archaeologists of the future may wonder what kind of game the people of the twentieth century played in a bowl so big.

There are provisions for overnight camping in Santa Fe Park on U.S. 67, on the east side of McCamey, and there is a scenic drive over the top of King Mountain. It is a county road, connecting U.S. 67 East with U.S. 385 Northwest.

CRANE COUNTY

Thousands of people traveled across what is now Crane County between the 1840s and the 1880s. None was tempted to stay. There were very few safe places to cross the Pecos River in the days before the bridges and dams. One of those places was here. The river forms the southwestern boundary of Crane County, and it is not a very impressive stream today. The Red Bluff Dam at the northern end of Reeves County has tamed the Pecos. But the river was a real obstacle to the Forty-niners and other early travelers. Many of the early wagon trains and stagecoaches came through Castle Gap in what is now Upton County and used the Horsehead Crossing in the southern end of what is now Crane County. Travelers using this crossing went north up the west bank of the Pecos almost to the New Mexico line and then turned west to El Paso in the earliest days. Most of the traffic steered a more westerly course from Horsehead after Fort Stockton and Fort Davis were built to protect the direct route from here to El Paso.

Horsehead Crossing was used by the Indians before the white man came here. They may have named it. Apparently the early white users thought the name was appropriate. Early

The wagon trains that came through Castle Gap in the 1840s and 1850s usually crossed the Pecos here at Horsehead Crossing. The Pecos is the boundary between Crane and Pecos counties. There is no access from the Crane County side, but there is from the Pecos County side, off Ranch Road 11.

accounts say there were always skeletons of horses and other animals lying around the river banks at the crossing. Wagon trains and cattle drivers often lost animals here. The Pecos crossing was a dreaded part of any trip across West Texas, and the water was not even good to drink. It tasted of salt and gypsum.

The lack of good water delayed settlement here and caused considerable inconvenience long after settlement began. The legislature created Crane County in 1887 from part of Tom Green County. It was named for William Carey Crane. He was a Baptist preacher. He came to Texas in 1863 to accept the presidency of Baylor University. The school was still at its original location in Independence, and having problems. Crane put a lot of energy and some of his own money into improving Baylor. He was president until he died in 1885, and his interest in education extended beyond Baylor. Crane was the first president of the Texas State Teachers' Association, and he helped persuade the legislature to establish the University of Texas and Sam Houston Normal Institute (now Sam Houston State University). The county seat is also named for Crane. It is the only town in the county. The present courthouse was built in 1958.

There were no more than 30 people in this whole county before the oil was discovered in 1925. The news of the oil brought the usual boom. Formal organization of the county was completed in 1927, and Crane was designated the county seat. Crane was a settlement of tin shacks and tents then. Old-timers tell of having to pay $2 or more for a barrel of water from the one good well in the sandhills outside town.

There has never been much farming in Crane County.

1   2

*1) Many Texas counties have more cows than people. Crane County has
more oil wells than people. The courthouse was built in 1958.*
*2) Crane and Crane County were named for William Carey Crane. He was an
early president of Baylor University.*
*3) Juan Cordona Lake near Crane once supplied a lot of salt for this area.
Now it is in the middle of one of the county's oil fields.*

3

There are some large sheep and cattle ranches here. But oil is
the big factor in the economy of Crane County. The county
usually ranks in the top four or five in the state in oil
production.

This is a county where the railroads had nothing to do with
the pattern of settlement. The Santa Fe line passes through
the extreme southeastern corner of the county, and the Texas
and Pacific cuts across the northwestern tip. Neither line ever
has had a stop in Crane County. The town of Crane has never
had rail service.

Crane County has a big natural salt deposit at Juan Cordona Lake, southwest of Crane. This was an important
source of table salt from the earliest days up until about 1930.

Oilmen feel at home on the golf course at the Crane Country Club. There are more than half a dozen oil wells on the fairways and greens. This arrangement is less wonderful than it might be because the club does not own the mineral rights.

WARD COUNTY

This county was also on one of the main routes used by travelers going to California between the 1840s and the 1880s, because one of the major Pecos River crossings was here. Emigrant Crossing was southwest of Monahans. This was the crossing Captain Randolph Marcy used when he explored the Staked Plain in 1849. The Butterfield stages used Emigrant Crossing for a time. The old crossing is several miles southeast of the present Interstate 20 bridge over the Pecos. It is on private property, and there is nothing at the site now to suggest that the crossing played any part in the development of the West.

Ward County was created from part of Tom Green County at the same time Crane County was formed in 1887. The county was named for Thomas William Ward. He was a native of Ireland. Ward came to Texas in 1835. He was a member of the little Texas force that took the Alamo from the Mexicans in December of that year. He lost a leg in that campaign. Ward held several offices in the days of the Republic. He was also the architect and the contractor for the building that housed the government of the Republic during the three years that Houston was the capital. Ward died in Austin 15 years before this county was created and named for him.

Ward County was settled several years before Crane County was. The Texas and Pacific Railroad was the main reason. Jay Gould was pushing the line westward from Fort Worth in the early 1880s as fast as he could, to link up with the Southern Pacific line C. P. Huntington was building eastward from California. The T&P laid its tracks diagonally across what was to become Ward County six years before the county was formed. Fewer than 100 people lived here when the county was created. But the population increased enough

1) Ward County was named for Thomas Ward. He was Irish and one of the heroes of the Texas Revolution. Ward lost his right leg in a fight with the Mexicans during the siege of the Alamo in 1835 and his right arm was blown away when a cannon he was manning during the 1841 celebration of Texas Independence Day misfired. He recovered from both mishaps and later held several public offices.

2) The original county seat was Barstow, but the first oil discoveries here were in the other end of the county. They drained the population away and the government moved to Monahans in 1938. A community center stands now on the square where the original courthouse stood.

3) The building the first bank built in Barstow is now the headquarters of the local irrigation district, but most of the downtown property here is vacant.

to justify formal organization by 1892. Barstow was designated the county seat when the county government was organized that year. Barstow is on the railroad at the western edge of the county, near the Pecos. There was some irrigation going on here and also around Grandfalls, farther down the Pecos, by the late 1890s. Barstow was named for George Barstow of Rhode Island. He financed the irrigation system.

Barstow had a lot going for it at the turn of the century. There was regular train service. The irrigation system made the farms along the Pecos productive. There were three churches, a hotel, a bank and an opera house in Barstow in 1910. Jay Gould's daughter, Ana, gave the town a library. The town of Monahans at that time had only about 200 people. Monahans is on the railroad at the northeastern corner of the county. The T&P made it a water stop when the tracks

1

2

1) The Ward County Courthouse is the original one built when the county government moved from Barstow to Monahans, but it has been enlarged.

2) The city of Monahans sits over an oil field. There are six pumps in this cluster at Main Street and Avenue A. These pumps are pumping oil from directional wells under various sections of the city. One of the wells is under the courthouse.

3) The section of desert known as the Monahans Sandhills stretches nearly 200 miles through Ward and Winkler counties. The Monahans Sandhills State Park takes in about 6 square miles of this strange area.

4) The pioneers first thought the sandhills area was a waterless wasteland. But the Indians knew, and the pioneers learned, that there is water underground here, fairly close to the surface in some places. There is moisture enough to support small groves of stunted oak trees. But the campground in Monahans Sandhills Park probably is the most desolate public campground in America.

3

4

1

1) *The bomber that dropped the first atomic bomb on Japan was once based at Pyote Field in Ward County. The plane was the Enola Gay.*
2) *The airmen called Pyote Field the Rattlesnake Bomber Base. The government closed it and sold the property in 1966. Part of the site is occupied now by a state home for children, but one of the big hangars is still standing south of the highway, west of Pyote. Some mementos of the base are preserved in a small museum in the Pyote Community Center.*

2

were laid in 1881 because a man named John Monahans had conveniently dug a water well. Oil was discovered in adjoining Winkler County in 1926. Monahans was the railroad town closest to the oil field, and it caught the economic fallout. The population jumped from 200 to 3,000. The Ward County seat moved from Barstow to Monahans in 1938. The present courthouse in Monahans was built in 1940 and enlarged in 1974.

There is another one of those big open oil storage reservoirs here, similar to the one outside McCamey. Shell built this one, just east of Monahans, in 1928, because construction of conventional tanks and pipelines could not keep up with oil production. This tank is about the same size as the one at Mc-Camey, designed to hold 1,000,000 barrels of crude. It had the same problems the McCamey project had. The concrete

1) A scientist in El Paso is trying to make alcohol for gasohol from tumbleweeds. It might be a new bonanza for this area. It is about as well supplied with tumbleweeds as it is with oil.

liner cracked and leaked. It never was filled. But it is still here, off U.S. 80, on the east side of Monahans.

The principal tourist attraction in Ward County is a few miles farther east. This is the Monahans Sandhills State Park. The park takes in only part of a vast area of shifting sand dunes resembling the Sahara. There is a museum and an interpretive center. There are provisions for picnicking, and the park has a number of campsites for rent. There is an admission fee. The address for reservations and further information is Box 1738, Monahans 79756.

LOVING COUNTY

This county was the last one in the state to be organized. It was created by the legislature in 1887 from part of Tom Green County. But there was not enough population to justify a county government until 1931. Loving County has more than 40 miles of frontage on the Pecos River. The river forms the western boundary of the county. And there is substantial oil production here. But there are very few people. The population was around 200 when the county was formally organized. It reached a high of almost 300 in 1940. But it has been declining since then. Fewer than 200 people live in Loving County now. There is only one town. It is Mentone, and it is the smallest county seat in Texas. The population is less than 50. There are two businesses in Mentone, one service station and one cafe. Mentone has highway connections to Pecos and Kermit, but there has never been a railroad here.

There is no school now operating in Loving County. Students all go to classes at Wink, in the next county, by bus. Births and deaths are rare in Loving County because there is no hospital in the county. There is no cemetery. There is no public debt, either. The oil fields give the county a healthy tax base, and the people here have never felt any need for expen-

1

1) This is the business district of Mentone, all of it. The Exxon station has a monopoly of the gas business and Newt Keen's Cafe gets all the eating and drinking business. Keen is a retired cowboy, still active as a story teller. Loving County has the smallest population of any county in Texas. Mentone is the smallest county seat and it is not growing.

2) A travel poster in the Mentone gas station depicts some of the beauty of the city of Menton, on the South Coast of France. Mentone apparently was named for Menton. At first glance, it might appear the two places have nothing in common except prickly pears. But there is not even that much similarity. The Texas Mentone has no prickly pears.

2

sive civic improvements. They regularly reject Washington's offers to share federal revenues with them.

There is a little farming here, and there are a few large ranches, but most of the income is from oil. It was discovered in 1925. Discovery of the Wheat Oil Field dictated the location of Mentone. The original settlement of this name was situated about ten miles from here. This settlement beside the Wheat Oil Field originally was called Ramsey. The settlers from the original Mentone moved here and brought the name Mentone with them. The present Loving County Courthouse was built in Mentone in 1935.

The town apparently was named for the city in France, but if there is any similarity, it is not readily apparent. The French city is an expensive resort on the Mediterranean, with every convenience and luxury. This Mentone lacks some basic necessities. The residents here have to have their drinking water hauled in from Pecos and Kermit.

Loving County was named for one of the earliest Texas trail drivers. Oliver Loving was born in Kentucky in 1812. He

1

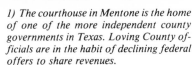

1) *The courthouse in Mentone is the home of one of the more independent county governments in Texas. Loving County officials are in the habit of declining federal offers to share revenues.*

2) *Sheriff Elgin Jones is also the tax collector. He's the only lawman in the county, but he says he can call in the Texas Rangers if he ever needs help.*

3) *The oldest building in Mentone is the community center. It was built in Porterville in 1910 as a church and moved here after a flood destroyed Porterville.*

4) *The Mentone school building has been vacant since 1978. The few school age children in the county go to classes in Wink by bus.*

3

4

came to Texas in 1845. Loving lived in Lamar County and in Collin County before he moved to Palo Pinto County and established a cattle business in 1855. Loving drove a herd of cattle to the Chicago stockyards in 1858. This is the earliest recorded instance of Texas cows being driven directly to northern markets. But there were some cases of Texas cows being driven to Louisiana earlier.

Oliver Loving was a pioneer rancher and trail driver. He blazed a trail to Chicago that later became known as the Shawnee Trail. He was the first to drive cows up what became the Western Trail and he and Charles Goodnight established the Goodnight-Loving Trail. Loving County was named for Oliver Loving.

Loving drove a herd to Denver in 1859. He almost got stranded there when the Civil War began. But he made his way back to Texas and supplied beef to the Confederate Army until the end of the war. Loving and his neighbor, Charles Goodnight, drove a herd of cattle from Palo Pinto County down through the South Plains, across the Pecos and through New Mexico to Colorado in 1866. This was the route that became known to history as the Goodnight-Loving Trail. Goodnight continued driving cattle and ranching until 1890. But Oliver Loving was killed by Indians on the Goodnight-Loving Trail in New Mexico in 1867, twenty years before the legislature created this county and named it for him.

WINKLER COUNTY
This is another one of the counties the legislature created when it carved up Tom Green County in 1887. The terrain is very similar to that in Ward County. The Monahans Sandhills extend into the southern part of Winkler County. Some people live here today by choice and praise the dry, invigorating climate. But the early travelers found nothing attractive about it. Water was scarce. The Indians were unfriendly. It was an area to be traversed as quickly as possible. A marker on State Highway 18, 12 miles south of Kermit, testifies to the hazards the early travelers encountered. The marker recalls that charred bones and scraps of metal found in 1901 indicate that a train of about 40 wagons was wiped out by Indians near here. The site of the apparent massacre is Willow Springs in the sandhills 6½ miles east of the highway.

Winkler County was named for Clinton M. Winkler. He came to Texas in 1840. He practiced law and served in the

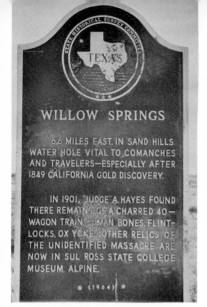

1

2

1) A wagon train apparently was wiped out by Indians here in southern
Winkler County sometime in the middle of the 19th Century. The assumption
is based on the discovery of some human bones and old hardware in the
desert southeast of Wink.
2) Winkler County is named for Judge Clinton Winkler. He was a member of
the Texas Court of Appeals when he died in 1882. He was a member of the
legislature and a Confederate officer before that.

state legislature before the Civil War. Winkler was a lieutenant colonel in the Confederate Army during the war. He
was a judge of the Court of Appeals from 1876 until he died
in 1882.

A few cattlemen came to the area that is now Winkler
County in the 1870s and 1880s. The Homestead Law of 1900
was supposed to encourage settlement of areas like this, but it
did not have much effect here. The law limited homesteaders
to four sections of land. Four sections of this land at that time
would not feed enough cows to support a family. The early
railroads missed the county. The 1890 census showed Winkler
county with a population of 18. The 1900 census showed an
increase to 60. Homesteading increased the population to
more than 400 by 1910, and formal organization of the county was completed that year.

The first post office in Winkler County was established in
1908 on the John Howe ranch, near the present city of Kermit. Some promoters tried to create a town around the post
office. They laid out some lots and advertised their new city
of Duval all over the country. A few of the lots were sold, but
Duval never became a town. The residents of the county

1

2

1) *The only town in Winkler County until 1926 was Kermit. It was designated the county seat when the county was organized in 1910. The first successful oil well in the county created a new town. It was named Wink and the people of Wink tried to get the county seat moved to their town. The proposition was voted down in 1927 and in 1929 and the courthouse was built in Kermit in 1929.*

2) *The early oil wells here were drilled with cable tool rigs and wooden derricks like this. This is the last wooden derrick used in the West Texas oil fields. It is on display in Pioneer Park in Kermit.*

3) *The pioneer home in Pioneer Park is furnished with antiques and open to the public on Sundays and by appointment. The location is East Avenue at School Street.*

3

The Winkler County oil boom of the 1920s created the town of Wink. It grew rapidly for a time, but people have been moving away from Wink in recent years. Many stores and business buildings are now vacant. There is no parking problem in downtown Wink.

voted in the election that established the county government to locate the county seat at Kermit. The post office moved to Kermit, too. Kermit was named for Kermit Roosevelt. He was Theodore Roosevelt's second son. Roosevelt was always inventing ways for his sons to develop grit and test their grit. One of his favorite ways was to have them visit frontier ranches. Kermit came here in about 1908 to hunt antelope with John Kayser and Frank Cowden on their T-Bar Ranch. The present courthouse was built in 1929 and worked over in 1973.

Kermit and Winkler County had five very lean years beginning in 1916. A severe drought sent most of the ranchers into bankruptcy. People moved away. The census of 1920 showed a population of 81 for the entire county.

The drought ended in 1922. Oil was discovered in the county in 1926, and the population increased substantially. Roy Westbrook drilled the discovery well on a ranch southwest of Kermit. The discovery created a new boom town in what had been a pasture. It was called Wink. This apparently is an abbreviation of the name of the county. Nobody had time to invent a new name. Wink reached a population of 4,000 by 1930. The population declined after that. It hovers, now, around 1,000. But development of the oil fields in the county continued on through the 1970s, and Winkler County still is one of the principal oil-producing counties in the state.

Some of the history of the county and the early years of the oil boom are preserved in Pioneer Park, in Kermit. There is a restored pioneer home with authentic furnishings and utensils. An old cable tool oil derrick is also on display.

A marker on State Highway 18, 10 miles north of Kermit, reminds us Texas once claimed a large part of New Mexico, Colorado, Wyoming and parts of Oklahoma and Kansas. The claim grew out of the treaty Texans forced Santa Anna to sign

1

1) Texas and New Mexico maintain small roadside parks where Texas State Highway 18 crosses the state line, north of Kermit. A marker here recalls that the boundary was established in 1850 when the U.S. government paid Texas $10 million to quit claiming that New Mexico was part of Texas.

2) There were a few Indian pictographs in a rock shelter on top of Blue Mountain but vandals and the elements have just about obliterated them. Blue Mountain is an outpost of the Llano Estacado on State Highway 302 east of Kermit.

2

after the Battle of San Jacinto. Santa Anna never thought so, but Texans claimed that agreement gave Texas nearly 100,000 square miles more territory than is included in the present boundaries of the state. The United States went to war with Mexico after Texas joined the union in 1845. The boundary dispute was one of the excuses for the war. The war ended when Mexico agreed to give up all claim to Texas, New Mexico, Arizona and California in exchange for $15 million. The United States then paid Texas $10 million to stop claiming lands beyond the boundaries we recognize today. The marker here recalls the agreement in 1850 that the boundary between Texas and New Mexico follows the 103rd Meridian down to the 32nd Parallel and then follows the 32nd Parallel westward to the Rio Grande.

ANDREWS COUNTY

This county was named for the first Texan killed in the revolution that made Texas independent of Mexico. There had been some skirmishing earlier, but it is generally accepted that the actual revolution began at Gonzales in October of

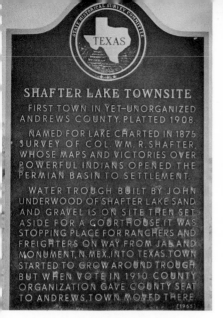

SHAFTER LAKE TOWNSITE

FIRST TOWN IN YET-UNORGANIZED
ANDREWS COUNTY. PLATTED 1908.

NAMED FOR LAKE CHARTED IN 1875
SURVEY OF COL. WM. R. SHAFTER
WHOSE MAPS AND VICTORIES OVER
POWERFUL INDIANS OPENED THE
PERMIAN BASIN TO SETTLEMENT.

WATER TROUGH BUILT BY JOHN
UNDERWOOD OF SHAFTER LAKE SAND
AND GRAVEL IS ON SITE THEN SET
ASIDE FOR A COURTHOUSE. IT WAS
STOPPING PLACE FOR RANCHERS AND
FREIGHTERS ON WAY FROM JAL AND
MONUMENT, N. MEX. INTO TEXAS. TOWN
STARTED TO GROW AROUND TROUGH
BUT WHEN VOTE IN 1910 COUNTY
ORGANIZATION GAVE COUNTY SEAT
TO ANDREWS, TOWN MOVED THERE.
(1965)

1   2

1) The original settlement in Andrews County has almost disappeared. The early settlers here built a town on the north shore of Shafter Lake but nearly everybody later moved to Andrews. This marker is on Farm Road 1967, west of U.S. 385. The town was on the opposite side of the road.
2) Shafter Lake is another one of the shallow salt lakes fairly common in this part of the Permian Basin.

1835 when Mexican troops tried to recover a cannon Mexican authorities had lent to the settlers there. The settlers refused to give up the cannon and attacked the Mexican soldiers. Richard Andrews was one of the Texans in that fight. He was wounded that day, and he was killed a few days later in a battle with Mexican troops at the Mission Concepción in San Antonio. The force Andrews went to San Antonio with was the force that compelled the Mexicans to surrender the Alamo in December of 1835. The Battle of Concepción was the first preliminary. It was fought October 28th. Sixty Mexicans were killed. Andrews was the only Texan killed. The legislature gave his name to this county when it was created from part of the old Bexar District in 1876.

The shortage of water and the surplus of Indians discouraged early settlement. The first town was Shafter Lake on the shore of the salt lake originally charted by Colonel William Shafter of the U.S. Army. The settlement of Shafter Lake began in the early 1900s. There was a post office by 1907. The town had two hotels, a bank, three churches and a school by 1910. The population was 400 or 500. But the newer town of

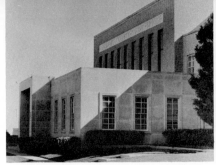

1

2

1) *The only building still standing at old Shafter Lake is the Irwin Ranch house on Farm Road 1967.*
2) *The courthouse built in Andrews in 1938 was modernized in 1960.*
3) *The Andrews County Museum is at 212 Northwest 2nd Street.*
4) *Andrews has a pleasant city park and lake six blocks west of U.S. 385. There is a free campground with hookups for a dozen trailers, restrooms and showers just one block south of the city park, on West Broadway at 6th.*

3

4

Andrews won the contest for the county seat when the county was formally organized in 1910. The people of Shafter Lake gradually moved to Andrews. Nothing is left of the town of Shafter Lake today except one building, a few foundations and a cemetery.

The great drought of 1916 set this county back as it did Winkler County. The population dropped from 975 in 1910 to 350 by 1920. It began to increase slowly again after 1920 and more rapidly after the oil was discovered in 1929. The population now is above 11,000. The city of Andrews has more than 10,000 people and one of the most prosperous school systems in the state, thanks to the oil. The present courthouse in Andrews was built in 1938 and overhauled in 1960.

The biggest salt lake in this part of the state is in Gaines County. This is Laguna Sabinas or Cedar Lake. Some of the salt used on the roads in the North in the winter is mined here.

There is some irrigation in Andrews County and some cotton and sorghum are grown here. Ranching produces more income than farming. But the income from the oil and gas leases and from the businesses servicing the petroleum industry is the biggest factor in the economy here by far. The median income in Andrews County is about as high as it is anywhere in the state.

The Andrews County Museum at 212 N. W. 2nd Street in Andrews has a collection of Indian relics, pictures and pioneer tools and implements on display.

There are provisions for camping near the Lakeside Park off State Highway 176, a few blocks west of U.S. 385. The campground has showers, restrooms and fireplaces.

GAINES COUNTY

The last great war chief of the Comanches may have been born in what is now Gaines County.

Quanah Parker became a chief of the Quahadi Comanches in about 1867. He carried on a guerilla war with the white settlers and U.S. troops in West Texas until 1875 when troops under Ranald Mackenzie finally crushed the Indian resistance. Parker and the Quahadis moved to a reservation in the Oklahoma Indian Territory, and there, in about 1877, Parker was chosen great chief of his tribe.

Quanah Parker's father was the Quahadi chief Peta Nocona. His mother was a white woman. Cynthia Ann Parker was kidnapped by Comanches from her parents' home at Parker's Fort, near the present city of Mexia, in 1836. Cynthia Ann was nine years old at the time. She lived with the Comanches until 1860 when Texas Rangers recaptured her during a skirmish in what is now Foard County. Cynthia Ann

1

2

1) Cedar Lake was a major Indian campground in the days when the Comanches controlled the Texas plains. The Comanches kept no records of births and deaths and so it can never be proven, but historians generally believe that Quanah Parker was born here.
2) Quanah Parker was the last great chief of the Comanches. He was only half Comanche. His mother was a white girl the Comanches had kidnapped. He got the name Parker from her.

gave birth to Quanah Parker sometime between 1845 and 1852. The date is uncertain and the place is, too. But Peta Nocona's tribe often camped on the shores of a big salt lake on the plains in what is now Gaines County. The Spanish called it Laguna Sabinas. It is labeled Cedar Lake on most maps today. The state of Texas put up a marker in 1936 recognizing the old Indian campground at Cedar Lake as the birthplace of Quanah Parker. The marker is on the north shore of the lake, on Farm Road 1066, 26 miles northeast of Seminole.

Cedar Lake is the largest alkali lake on the Texas plains. It covers ten sections, but it rarely has more than two or three inches of water in it. The water is salty and not fit to drink. But there were fresh water springs at the north and south ends of the lake in the early days. There was plenty of good grass to attract the buffalo, and the Indians camped here regularly for generations. Oil was discovered in the area in the 1930s, and the lake is dotted now with wells.

The Indians had this area pretty much to themselves until the white buffalo hunters and Mackenzie's soldiers crowded them out in the middle 1870s. Cattlemen began moving in about 1880. Most of the land was open range until about 1900 when the railroads and the school districts the state had awarded it to began selling it off to homesteaders.

1

2

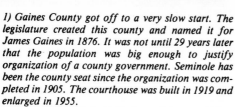

1) Gaines County got off to a very slow start. The legislature created this county and named it for James Gaines in 1876. It was not until 29 years later that the population was big enough to justify organization of a county government. Seminole has been the county seat since the organization was completed in 1905. The courthouse was built in 1919 and enlarged in 1955.

2) Some relics and photographs of the early ranches and oil fields are preserved in a small museum in the Gaines County Library building on U.S. 180, just west of downtown Seminole.

3) The original meeting place for settlers in this area was this grove of trees in a draw just south of the present town of Seminole. Hackberry Grove was a recreation area for years after the residents built other places for their meetings. But it is a pipeline station, now, and closed to the public.

3

The first white settlers probably were members of the C. C. Medlin family. They settled in 1881 at Hackberry Grove in a draw just south of the present town of Seminole. Mackenzie's troops had reported the rare stand of large hackberry trees at this site when they made their first survey trip here in 1871. The trees were nourished by underground water. The troops reported finding several dozen shallow wells here and in nearby Seminole Draw, apparently dug by the Indians.

The legislature separated this county from the Bexar District in 1876 and named it for James Gaines. He was an early settler in East Texas. Gaines was one of the signers of the Declaration of Independence, and he served in the congress of the Republic. He went to California during the gold rush of 1849, and he died there in 1856, twenty years before this county was created.

There were no whites living in Gaines County when it was created. Census figures show a population of eight whites in 1880. The number of settlers increased to 68 by 1890, and

1) Two big carbon black plants operated at Seagraves for a number of years but both plants have now been closed down. These plants burned natural gas and collected carbon from the smoke. The more smoke, the better for the carbon business. But the smoke and soot from the plants caused a lot of complaints and sometimes blackened the cotton in the fields around the plants. The complaints and damage claims and the rising cost of natural gas forced the closing of the plants.

2) Seagraves has lost some population and there are several vacant buildings around the Museum and Art Center on Main Street just west of U.S. 385.

2

there were enough people by 1905 to complete the organization of a county government.

The first meeting to discuss formation of a county government was held under the trees in Hackberry Grove. The citizens voted to locate the county seat on a site about a mile north of the grove. The Gaines County Historical Survey Committee's *Gaines County Story* says the site of the town that became Seminole was donated by a syndicate of New York investors. The present courthouse was built in 1919 and enlarged in 1955.

The name Seminole apparently was chosen by the U.S. Post Office Department from a list of suggestions the founders of the town submitted. The suggestion surely was inspired by Seminole Draw where some of those Indian wells were found. There was a band of Seminoles in West Texas at one time, and the draw may have been named for them, but it is more likely it was named for Ranald Mackenzie's Seminole Indian Scouts.

The Midland and Northwestern Railroad reached Seminole in 1918. But the area was in a serious economic slump because of drought and severe winter weather. The railroad failed.

1

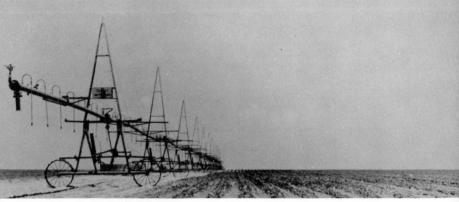

3

2

1) Cotton has been a major crop in Texas since the 1880s. Much of it now is grown on the West Texas plains, and Gaines County is one of the major producers. Raising cotton on the plains is nothing like it was in the plantation days. All the cultivating and planting is done by big, expensive machines.

2) The fields stretch to the horizon and the crops are watered by automatic sprinklers. These sprinkling rigs draw their water from underground wells and some of the rigs are half a mile long.

3) The foliage is killed with chemicals after the bolls open and the bolls are harvested by mechanical strippers.

The T&P took over the line and provided rail service between Midland and Seminole briefly, but the T&P abandoned the line in 1925.

The Santa Fe extended a line from Lubbock into Gaines County in 1917. This line terminated at the Blythe Ranch.

The city of Odessa apparently was named for a city in Russia. But Ector County was named for an adopted Texan. Matthew Ector came to Texas from Georgia too late for the revolution but in time to distinguish himself in the Civil War. He was a brigadier general in the Confederate Army and he was wounded in the fighting for Atlanta. Ector lived in Marshall and Tyler and probably never was in this part of Texas.

The settlement that developed at the terminus was first named Blythe, but the railroad changed the name to Seagraves to honor one of the railroad officials. This line survived the drought. Seagraves was the busiest cattle shipping point in the country for a time because it was the railhead closest to many of the ranches in West Texas and eastern New Mexico. Seagraves had a population of 8,000 at the height of the boom that followed the oil discoveries in Gaines County in the 1930s. About 2,000 people live in Seagraves now.

The people of Gaines County had some lean years during the droughts of 1916 and the 1930s. But the hard times taught the farmers here how to plow their land deeper and forced them to use the underground water for irrigation. They have more than 400,000 acres under irrigation now. The crops of cotton, wheat, sorghums, peanuts and vegetables earn millions of dollars a year. The cattle and sheep earn millions more, and the oil production is worth hundreds of millions.

It took tough people to survive the early years, but the survivors found it was worth it.

ECTOR COUNTY

This county has some of the most prolific oil wells in the country. Only a couple of other counties produce more oil. The oil was discovered here in 1926. The population of the city of Odessa immediately doubled, and it has been growing almost constantly ever since. More than 80,000 people now live in Odessa, and the city has one of the largest inland petrochemical complexes in the nation.

1) *Odessa got its start the same way Midland did, as a stop on the Texas and Pacific Railroad. The Ector County Courthouse here was built in 1964.*
2) *The jackrabbit statue by the Odessa Chamber of Commerce building at 400 North Lincoln is not as much a monument to the rabbits as it is a monument to a publicity stunt. The publisher of the Odessa newspaper invented a jackrabbit roping contest to promote the Odessa Rodeo in 1932.*

This is another one of the counties carved out of Tom Green County, after Tom Green County was separated from the original Bexar County. The original Bexar County included all of West Texas. The area that Bexar County originally covered is now divided into 128 counties. The original Tom Green County, as established in 1874 from part of Bexar County, included all of the area that is now included in Tom Green, Coke, Sterling, Irion, Reagan, Glasscock, Midland, Upton, Crane, Ward, Loving, Winkler and Ector counties.

Nothing much was happening here when the legislature fixed the boundaries and named this county for Judge Matthew D. Ector. That was in 1887. Judge Ector had died eight years earlier. He had come to Texas from Georgia in 1850. He served in the Texas legislature before the Civil War. He rose from private to brigadier general in the Confederate Army during the war, and he was presiding judge of the State Court of Civil Appeals when he died in 1879.

Captain Marcy's expedition came through here in 1849, and many of the emigrant wagon trains came this way. But the area was still unsettled when the Texas and Pacific work crews showed up in 1881 to lay the tracks for the line from Fort Worth to El Paso. The rail line more or less followed the original Marcy Trail from Big Spring to the Pecos River. It cut diagonally across the southern half of Ector County. There were a few cow camps, but no towns. The railroad crews built their own work camps as they moved across the plain. One of those work camps became the city of Odessa.

1) *The University of Texas of the Permian Basin opened in 1973. The new school occupies a 600-acre campus at University and Parkway in Odessa.*
2) *The Globe of the Great Southwest is a theater on the campus of Odessa College.*
3) *The theater is an almost exact replica of the building where William Shakespeare presented his plays in London in the 16th Century.*

The railroad workers named it. They supposedly chose the name because some of them came from Russia, and they thought the plains here resembled the plains around the Russian city of Odessa.

The railroad dug wells and brought in windmills, and soon there were a few settlers. Velma Barrett and Hazel Oliver say in their book *Odessa, City of Dreams* that one of the first settlers was an eccentric prospector named Ben Sublett. He led people to believe he had found gold somewhere in the area, and he occasionally displayed a few gold nuggets, but he died without telling anybody where he got them.

The T&P circulated some promotional literature in the late 1880s touting Odessa as a coming agricultural area. The pamphlets claimed the town had a year-around climate so

1

1) *The Presidential Museum has a large collection of portraits and cartoons of presidents and vice presidents of the United States and campaign paraphernalia from many of the campaigns of the past. The museum is in the Ector County Library building at 7th and Lee. It is open weekdays and free.*

2) *The Museum of Time and Travel has a collection of old cars and old timepieces. The museum has a Cadillac once owned by Shirley Temple and a watch once owned by Benjamin Franklin. There is an admission fee.*

3) *The great Odessa Meteor Crater is largely silted in, now, but people still come to see it.*

2

3

1) The oldest building in Odessa is the house Charles White built in 1887 at what is now 112 East Murphy Street. The old house was neglected for a long time, but the Ector County Historical Commission has it now, and it is going to be restored.

2) One of the attractions for children in the Prairie Pete Park is a colony of prairie dogs. This is part of Sherwood Park at 44th and Dixie. The prairie dogs once were such a nuisance on the plains here that the legislature passed a law making it legal to poison them.

good it would cure invalids. They claimed there were no mosquitoes and no Indians within 300 miles. They promised plenty of underground water and spoke of the possibility of growing fruits and grapes. The promoters said the town of Odessa was an especially suitable place for families because there were deed restrictions to ensure there never would be any saloons. The town had two stores and one small hotel and a post office in 1891.

The sheriff and a partner broke the deed restrictions and opened a saloon. The area proved to be better suited to ranching than to farming and so Odessa became a cow town. Other saloons opened and Odessa had quite a reputation for rowdiness for a while. Prohibition changed that, and the discovery of the oil changed nearly everything else about Odessa. Ector County has produced more than 2 billion barrels of oil from land that was selling for $2 to $4 an acre when the railroad was trying to entice people here in the 1880s.

The city is headquarters now for several natural gas companies, carbon black plants and rubber and nylon factories, and for many manufacturing and service concerns related to the oil industry.

Odessa is the home of the University of Texas of the Permian Basin. The city has its own symphony orchestra and a Civic Music Association. Plays are presented regularly in the Globe of the Great Southwest on the grounds of Odessa College. The Globe is a replica of William Shakespeare's Globe Theater.

1

2

3

1) *Much of the landscape around Odessa looks like this. Few inland cities anywhere have such a concentration of petrochemical plants. Few cities are as close to such a big supply of petroleum.*

2) *A surplus railroad depot from Pecos has become part of a restaurant on U.S. 385 across from Odessa College.*

3) *The lack of trees gave this settlement its name. A community has to have a name if it's going to have a post office, so the original settlers here submitted the name Notrees. The Post Office accepted the name. Then the settlers did some planting. Notrees now has a few trees, maybe more than people.*

The Odessa Meteor Crater is the second biggest such crater ever found in the United States. It is off U.S. 80 about eight miles southwest of Odessa. The crater is about 500 feet across. It was probably 100 feet deep at one time, but it is now mostly filled with silt. The meteor hit here about 20,000 years ago.

There is a town at the western edge of Ector County named Notrees. The name described the landscape at the time the post office was established in 1944. But people have been improving the landscape since then. Notrees now has enough trees to be called something else. But it is still called Notrees.

People unaccustomed to driving in West Texas may be surprised to find other drivers hailing them. It only happens on the secondary roads. Drivers in plain American cars or pickup trucks will lift two or three fingers from their steering wheels just before their vehicles meet yours. West Texans have been doing this since horse and buggy days. It just means, "Howdy." They are not offended if you don't respond, but you probably will. It's contagious.

Index

Bold type represents the location of a related photograph.

Church 141; First Methodist Church
141; Colorado Opera House **139**, 141;
Arnett house 141; Coleman house 141;
Hardegree house 141; Burns house 141;
Majors house 141; Colorado City
Museum 141, **141**
Communistic Colony of Bettina: 49, 113
Concho County: 94
Concho River: 94, **95**
Concordia Lutheran College: 14
Content: 94
Council House Fight: 6
Crane: 167-68
   Courthouse **168**
Crane County: 166
Crane, William Carey: 167, **168, 170**
Crouch, Hondo: 60
Custer, Gen. George Armstrong: **7**, 8

D
Dalton Gang: 103
Daughters of the Confederacy: 13
Daughters of the Republic of Texas: 13
Davis, Gov. Edmund Jackson: 9, **9**, 10,
67, 87
Davis, Jefferson: 65
Dawson County: 127
Dawson Massacre: 128
Dawson, Nicholas Mosby: 127-28

E
Earl of Aylesford: 122-23
East Texas Oil Field: 161
Ector County: 188
Ector, Matthew D.: **188**, 189
Eden: 96
Eden, Fred: 96
Eldorado: 113-15
   Courthouse **114**; Jail **115**
Episcopal Theological Seminary of the
Southwest: 14
Enchanted Rock State Natural Area: 49,
51, **51**
Evers, Marvin: **51**

F
Ficklin, Ben: 82
Fisher-Miller Grant: 95
Florence: 32
Fort Concho: **83**, 85, 87
Fort Chadbourne: 87-88, **87**
Fort Mason: 105-6, **105**
Fort McKavett: 101-2, **101**
Fredericksburg: 52-59
   Courthouse 52, **52**; Library 52, **52**;
Pioneer Museum **53**, 56; Nimitz Hotel
54, 57; Vereins Kirche 54, **54**; Admiral
Nimitz Center 57; Zion Lutheran
Church **56**, 57; White Elephant Saloon
56, 57; Loeffler-Weber house **56**, 59;
Admiral Nimitz birthplace 59;
Montgomery log cabin 59; Knopp house
59

Friday Mountain: **76**
Friday Mountain Ranch: 76
   Johnson Institute 76; Friday Mountain
Boys' Camp 76

G
Gail: **132-33**
   Courthouse **132**, 133; Jail **132**; County
Museum 133, **133**
Gaines County: 183
Garden City: 149
   Courthouse **149**; Jail **149**
Garrett, Herman: 156-58
Georgetown: 31-32
   Courthouse **30**, 31; Inner Space Cavern
32, 32; Mar-Jon Candle Factory 32;
Shafer Saddle Shop 32; Dimmit building
30, 32; Dimmit house 32; G. W. Riley
house 32
Gillespie County: 52
   Cherry Spring Church **60**
Gillespie, Richard Addison: 52
Glasscock county: 148
Glasscock, George Washington: 31,
148-49
Glickman, O.: **124**
Goodfellow Air Force Base: **86**
Goodnight-Loving Trail: 96
Gorman Falls: **46**
Granite Mountain at Marble Falls: 12, 37
Green, Thomas: 81
Grierson Spring: **147**, 148
Guion, David: 93

H
Hackberry Grove: 185-86, **185**
Hamilton, Andrew J.: 7
Hamilton Pool: **24**
Hannig, Susana Dickinson: 20
Harrell, Joseph: 3
Hayrick: 88
   Hayrick Cemetery **88**
Hays, Capt. John Coffee (Jack): 51-52,
72-73, **74**
Hays County: 71
Higgins-Horrell Feud: 40-41
Hill Country Arts Foundation: 63, **63**
Hill Country Fine Arts Trail Program: 63
Hoodoo War: 106
Hornsby, Reuben: 3
Hornsby, Rogers: 3
Horsehead Crossing: 166-67, **167**
Houston, Sam: **4**, 5-7
Houston, Sen. Temple: **11**, 12
Howard County: 120
Howard, Volney Erskine: 91, **121**, 122
Hunt: 64
   River Inn 64, **64**
Huston-Tillotson College: 14
Hutchins City: 92

I
Inks Lake: **36**

Photo Credits:

All of the photographs for this book, with the exception of those listed below, were made by Ray Miller, Gary James, Bill Springer, John Treadgold, Mark Williams and Jon Burkhart and processed and printed by Fred Edison.

The first number indicates the page, the second number indicates the number of the photograph on that page.

Alamo Museum: 100-1
Big Spring Herald: 123-2, 127-1 (Bill Forshee)
Classic Car Showcase: 65-1
Colorado City Museum: 138
Fort Concho Museum: 81-2
Goodyear Tire and Rubber Company: 85
Haley History Center: 159-2
Houston Public Library: 4-1-2, 7, 9-1-2, 25-1, 26-1, 29-2, 44-1-3, 62-1, 74-3, 80, 83-2, 88-3, 94, 96-2, 98, 102, 112-2, 131-2, 135-1, 142-1, 145-2, 150-2, 168-2, 176, 177-2
Library of Congress: 81-1
Lyndon B. Johnson Library: 57 (Frank Wolfe)
Longhorn Cavern State Park: 35-2
Midland Chamber of Commerce: 156
Midland County Library: 157-1-3
Miers Museum, Sonora: 114-3
Permian Historical Society, UTPB: 188
Scurry County Museum: 136-2
Smithsonian Institution: 184-2
Texas A&M: 187-3 (James E. Vance)
Texas Legislative Council: 3, 4-3, 8-2, 11-1-2-3
Texas State Library: 40, 120-2, 121-1
U.S. Air Force: 23 (TSGT Gary Smith), 172
Wonder World, San Marcos: 73-1